Waters of Africa

MANAGING EDITORS

Amy Bauman
Barbara J. Behm

CONTENT EDITORS

Amanda Barrickman
James I. Clark
Patricia Lantier
Charles P. Milne, Jr.
Katherine C. Noonan
Christine Snyder
Gary Turbak
William M. Vogt
Denise A. Wenger
Harold L. Willis
John Wolf

ASSISTANT EDITORS

Ann Angel
Michelle Dambeck
Barbara Murray
Renee Prink
Andrea J. Schneider

INDEXER

James I. Clark

ART/PRODUCTION

Suzanne Beck, Art Director
Andrew Rupniewski, Production Manager
Eileen Rickey, Typesetter

Library of Congress Cataloging-in-Publication Data

Fornasari, Lorenzo, 1960-
  [Acque d'Africa. English]
  Waters of Africa / Lorenzo Fornasari, Anja Roese.

  — (World nature encyclopedia)
  Translation of: Acque d'Africa.
  Includes index.
  Summary: Describes the plant and animal life of the
waters of Africa and its interaction with the environment.
  1. Aquatic ecology—Africa—Juvenile literature. 2. Biotic
communities—Africa—Juvenile literature. [1. Aquatic
animals—Africa. 2. Aquatic plants—Africa. 3. Ecology—
Africa. 4. Africa.] I. Roese, Anja, 1954-.
II. Title. III. Series: Natura nel mondo. English.
QH194.F6713 1988   574.5′263′096—dc19   88-18387
ISBN 0-8172-3325-3

Cover Photo: J.C. Stevenson—Animals Animals

WORLD NATURE ENCYCLOPEDIA

Waters of Africa

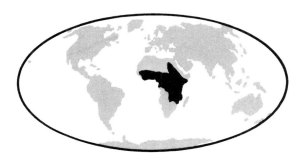

Lorenzo Fornasari
Anja Roese

RAINTREE
STECK-VAUGHN
L I B R A R Y

Austin, Texas

CONTENTS

INTRODUCTION

All life-forms have always been tied closely to the availability of water. Only a few plant and animal species with special adaptations are able to survive the difficult conditions of dry environments. It is not surprising that most of the animals in Africa, and in the world, are found in large flood plains. They live close to rivers and lakes.

In Africa, water transforms savannahs, or treeless plains. Plains that are almost sterile become fertile grasslands. Water allows the growth of lush forests along rivers in one of the hottest regions on earth. These beautiful riverbank forests, called "gallery forests," are extensions of equatorial forest environments. Numerous herds of antelope and gazelles are able to live here.

The African continent is a land of many contrasts. There is an incredible difference between areas that are near bodies of water and the vast Sahara and Kalahari deserts. Extremely arid areas alternate with extremely fertile ones.

The Nile is the most outstanding African river. It flows from the wild and fertile interior regions of Africa to the Mediterranean Sea and its age-old settlements. This river is a natural bridge across the desert. It is a route followed by birds during migrations. It is also an "access road" and an important point of reference for travelers. Three thousand years ago, this river route was traveled by traders of elephant tusks. The tusks were taken from elephants hunted in the southern plains. Many explorers also followed the course of the Nile in their quest to chart unknown lands of Africa's interior. To explorers, the untouched fertile lands seemed like unexpected wonders. They were surprised by the variety of unusual animals that inhabited these lands.

Today elephants, rhinoceroses, zebras, and a thousand other animal species still share these open spaces. However, they do not venture far from the bodies of water which they visit regularly. Antelope and gazelles drink alongside lions and cheetahs. While drinking, animals are not usually in danger of being attacked by predators. Lions and cheetahs prey on animals elsewhere, away from the water. Near the water there is a "truce" that not even hyenas dare to break.

Africa's vast lowland plains are populated by herds and herds of *herbivores* (plant-eaters). Lakes and rivers provide water, the basis for life on the grasslands. Marshes and temporary ponds created by heavy rains are inhabited by large migrating birds. These birds fly to Africa from Eurasia for the winter. Other birds migrate here from other areas of the African continent to escape the dry season.

A BRIEF HISTORY AND GEOGRAPHY

For Europeans and peoples of Western cultures, the history of Africa began in the 1400s. During these years, several geographic discoveries were made by exploration parties.

Prior to the 1400s, the Egyptian and Arab civilizations along the Mediterranean Sea were already well known. But culturally speaking, Africa was the "Dark Continent" because it was unexplored. It remained the land of great equatorial forests, huge lakes, and the richest animal populations in the world. The Egyptian cities of Cairo and Alexandria were as far from Africa's interior as from Rome, Italy, and Athens, Greece.

The Egyptians and the Black Civilizations

The ancient Romans and Greeks learned about African regions south of the Sahara Desert through the Egyptians. The Greek historian Herodotus traveled to Egypt in 450 B.C. He wrote of a country beyond the desert, where the people were small and black, and a large river with crocodiles ran from west to east.

It was natural that the Egyptians would be curious about the regions where their great Nile River originated. They owed the development of their civilization to the river. The Nile was responsible for the fertility of their lands. Each flooding season, the river carried fertile deposits of silt into their fields.

In 1200 B.C., Ramses II, pharaoh of ancient Egypt, knew of the existence of Lake Albert, Lake Victoria, and Murchison Falls. In 600 B.C., the Egyptian king Necho II organized an expedition of Phoenician sailors. They attempted to sail completely around the continent of Africa, leaving from the Red Sea. In spite of continuous efforts, explorers were unable to make their way beyond the Sahara Desert. Africa's interior lands were protected by the desert. And they were protected by the people who controlled the only access, the Nile River.

The Nile can only be navigated in certain sections. This is because it is interrupted by a series of six *cataracts*, or waterfalls. These cataracts block the passage of boats. Near these cataracts, flourishing cultures developed. People of these cultures traded with Egypt. Occasionally, they also had military conflicts with Egyptian soldiers.

Egyptians reached the fourth cataract around 1500 B.C., during the period of their greatest power. But they were unable to travel beyond that point. This was the land of the

9

This map shows the human population density for the African continent. In the hot climates of Africa, water is important for the survival of plants and animals. It is also needed for the survival and expansion of human settlements. The major African civilizations of the past developed along large rivers. Even today, population density is related to the presence of water. The most densely-populated zones are found along the Nile River. An advanced Egyptian culture developed along this great river.

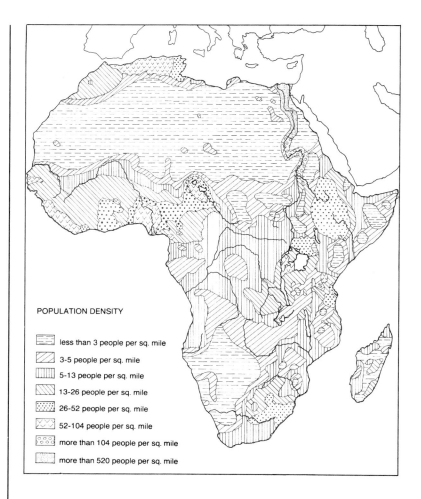

POPULATION DENSITY

	less than 3 people per sq. mile
	3-5 people per sq. mile
	5-13 people per sq. mile
	13-26 people per sq. mile
	26-52 people per sq. mile
	52-104 people per sq. mile
	more than 104 people per sq. mile
	more than 520 people per sq. mile

Nubians, the people of several Negroid tribes. They lived in the area that is now southern Egypt and northern Sudan. The Nubians traded gold, ivory, and ebony wood that came from Africa's mysterious southern forests.

According to French historian Pierre Bertaux, the techniques of working with iron, copper, gold, and brass spread from Meroë, the ancient capital of Nubia, to all other parts of Africa. These metal-working techniques supported formation of several small, scattered settlements of people. The settlements were stable organizations with complex and effective governing systems. In the ancient Congolese reigns, the people of a settlement regard a blacksmith as a "founding father." Today, blacksmiths still enjoy high status throughout Africa.

In the first centuries after Christ, a loose trade network connected the most developed areas of the African conti-

The beautiful scenery of the Congo River is seen near Crystal Mountains in Zaire. A short distance from here, the river flows into the Atlantic Ocean. Unlike most other African rivers, the flow of the Congo River remains fairly constant throughout the year. This is made possible by tributaries flowing from both the north and south. When the waters of the northern tributaries are low, the waters of the southern tributaries are high, and vice versa. When the region of the northern tributaries has a wet season, the region of the southern tributaries undergoes a dry season. This assures a continuous supply of water to the Congo River.

nent. These areas included the eastern Sudan of the Nubians. They included Chad, where the Nok and Ife cultures developed along the bank of the Niger River. And they included prosperous Ghana, which developed near the Senegal River.

Meroë, the ancient capital of Nubia, dominated Nubian culture for about a thousand years. It was replaced by the black Christian reigns of the cataracts. These settlements were of the Eastern Orthodox faith. They survived until the last Crusades.

Although unknown to Europeans, the "Dark Continent" was not backward or isolated. In Zanzibar, for example, merchants traded with distant lands. Coins minted in both the Roman Empire and in China provide evidence of extensive trade with foreign merchants. Merchants sailed from all parts of the world in order to buy products from Africa's interior areas, such as Lake Albert and Lake Tanganyika.

From the Middle Ages to the 1500s, Ghana was the main supplier of gold for all of the Mediterranean countries. Gold was transported by caravans that crossed the western Sahara Desert. This transport stands as evidence of the long and profitable contacts between Mediterranean and African civilizations.

The European Explorations

The Europeans did not become interested in Africa

Hippopotamuses wade in Lake Albert. The landscape is as wild today as it appeared to the eyes of Samuel Baker, the first European explorer in the area. Baker reached the lake by following the Nile River upstream. The story of the exploration and colonization of Africa by Europeans is full of adventure. It includes political scheming and the greedy pursuit of economic interests.

until the fifteenth century. During that century, Portuguese navigators sailed along the western coast of Africa and reached the Canary Islands. They were followed by the French, who sailed around the Cape Verde Islands. By the fifteenth century, the Mediterranean culture of Africa had been converted to the Moslem religion. European governments sent out exploration parties because they wished to trade directly with the Africans, rather than through Mediterranean middlemen.

The Portuguese sailed around Africa to find a route to the East Indies. They persisted in this aim throughout the fifteenth century. They did not explore Africa's interior.

However, they partially explored the basin of the Congo River. In 1485, Portuguese explorer Diego Cao sailed partway up the Congo River with an expedition of three light sailing ships. The Portuguese colonized Africa's interior by converting the people who lived along the Congo River to Christianity. They also established diplomatic relations between the kings of Portugal and the rulers of the Congo.

Another exploration effort occurred along the Senegal River. This was undertaken by a French trading company. The trading company appointed Thomas Lambert to lead the expedition. In 1638, Lambert reached the mouth of the river. He sailed upstream for over 124 miles (200 kilometers) to the city of Podor. Following this expedition, the French extended their influence even further into the interior.

African settlements were located near the courses of rivers. Missionaries, explorers, and colonists used these rivers as the main routes to penetrate Africa's interior. However, exploration did not take place on a large scale until 1800. About this time, the English became interested in the delta of the Niger River. They also moved up the Gambia River into the interior of Africa.

By 1855, no one had yet explored the area where the Nile River originated. The only available information on the region was based on a report by two German missionaries. They reached the area several years before. They told of tall mountains with peaks that were always covered with snow. They were describing Mount Kilimanjaro and Mount Kenya.

Finding the sources of the Nile River was a goal of exploration for the English and the Italians. The Italian Giovanni Miani set out from Egypt, but he was continually delayed by the Egyptian government. The Royal Geographic Society sent out an exploratory mission that left Zanzibar in 1857. The expedition was commanded by Richard Burton and John Speke. It reached Lake Tanganyika in 1858. Speke and an interpreter continued further into the interior and discovered Lake Victoria. In 1860, Speke and James Grant returned with a second expedition. They completely circled the lake. They were able to identify with certainty that Lake Victoria was one of the sources of the Nile River.

In the meantime, another Englishman, Samuel Baker, left Egypt and proceeded upstream along the Nile River. In 1864, Baker discovered a lake that he named Albert, in honor of Queen Victoria's husband. The lake was located only 62 miles (100 km) beyond the point where Italian

explorer Miani had stopped. Farther south, David Livingstone discovered Lake Nyasa. Several years later, Henry Stanley and Livingstone explored the area of Lake Tanganyika. Stanley later discovered the origin of the Congo River, which he navigated to the source. It was a voyage that lasted three years. Following this discovery, Stanley was given an assignment by King Leopold II of Belgium. He was to open a route along the river and to negotiate treaties with local rulers.

During those years, various countries were competing to discover new African territories. The continent was crossed far and wide by agents of various European governments. These agents noted geographic discoveries. They also made commercial and political agreements with native rulers and tribes they encountered.

Europeans viewed expansion into Africa as a great economic opportunity. As a result, a "gold rush" atmosphere prevailed in 1885, just before the Conference of Berlin. This conference was held to sanction various colonial zones in Africa which were under the control of European countries. The British sent an agent to finalize official agreements with

Livestock drink along the left bank of the Nile River. The dryness of the soil just a short distance from the river shows the importance of the river for agriculture and livestock raising. The Nile is the only water supply for a tremendously large land area. Its fertile deposits of silt fill the needs of agriculture and livestock raising in lands nearby.

The Niger River, in Mali, is seen during the dry period. The Niger is as important for western Africa as the Nile is for northeastern Africa. Its periodic floods provide local people with the necessary resources for survival.

the natives in the delta of the Niger River. They hoped an agreement could be finalized before the French claimed the area. However, the British agent reached the Niger delta five days too late. A protectorate treaty had already been signed between the native authorities and the German government.

All of this travel and exploration into the African interior was not easy. Many of the animals used to carry explorers' loads were killed by disease carried by the tse-tse fly. Thus, explorers had to use human bearers to carry their loads. These bearers had to be cared for, too. Often they had to be guarded so that they would not run away. The explorers and bearers were afflicted with various diseases. And often, traveling groups were forced to pay tolls to local authorities. The practice of charging tolls was devised by clever natives. They had centuries of experience in dealing with caravans of Arab slave traders.

The Lakes and Rivers of the Continent

The Nile is the longest river in the world. Including the Kagera River, which flows into Lake Victoria from the plateau of Tanganyika, the Nile covers a distance of 4,136 miles (6,671 km). It extends from the equator to the Mediterranean

Sea. The Nile flows from Lake Victoria to Lake Kyoga in central Uganda. From there it flows into Lake Albert. The river then flows to Sudan, where it is called the White Nile. The White Nile unites with the Blue Nile at Khartoum, Sudan. The many branches and tributaries of the Nile were mapped in 1937.

The Nile is extremely important because it drains a basin of 1,100,000 square miles (2,850,000 sq. km). It drains a region characterized by very few bodies of water. During the summer, tropical rains cause the Nile to swell. The river then floods an area of 13,510 sq. miles (35,000 sq. km). It fertilizes dry areas with silt carried in its waters. Today, this flooding is artificially controlled. Dams form large artificial reservoirs and lakes. The most important lake is Lake Nasser. It occupies 1,930 sq. miles (5,000 sq. km) and is formed by the Aswan Dam.

The flooding seasons of the Niger River are also important. Silt carried by this river is not as fertile as silt carried by the Nile. Niger River silt fertilizes lands used by the Fulbe shepherds for grazing their herds. The Niger's course crosses an area of forests characterized by heavy rainfall. When it floods, the water covers an area of 10,000 sq. miles (26,000 sq. km). The upper course of the Niger River crosses a humid and relatively cool region that favors the growth of rich crops.

The Niger River originates in the Fouta Djallon Mountains of Guinea. Many rivers of western Africa also originate in this mountainous region. Of these, the Senegal, Gambia, and Konkouré rivers are the most important.

Some African river basins lie close to each other in certain areas. For example, during the dry season the Logore River flows north into Lake Chad. But during the rainy season, its waters overflow into the Benue River. The Benue River, in turn, flows southwest into the Niger River. The Niger River then empties into the Atlantic Ocean.

In the past, the Niger River flowed into an interior depression in the Sahara Desert. Its course has changed with time. Presently, the river's course takes the shape of a semicircle. It curves first to the northeast and then to the southeast. The Niger River, which empties into the Gulf of Guinea, is the third longest African river. It is 2,585 miles (4,160 km) long.

A map showing population densities also shows the importance of African rivers. In Africa, the distribution of human settlements is closely related to the location of sur-

Opposite page: The majestic Victoria Falls is one of the most spectacular sights in all of Africa. The cascades interrupt the course of the Zambesi River before it flows into the Indian Ocean. The Zambesi is the longest river in southern Africa.

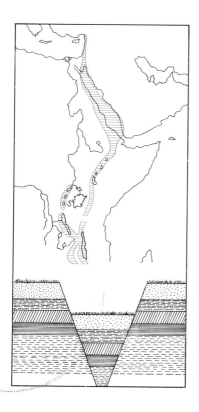

The large, natural crack of the Rift Valley was formed when two plates of the earth's crust separated from each other. This caused a sinking of the land in the area between two faults, producing a long, narrow depression, or valley. The conditions at the bottom of the valley favor the gathering of surface water. As a result, the Rift Valley contains several of Africa's largest lakes. The valley begins near the mountains of Turkey, crosses the Red Sea, and ends in the area facing Madagascar.

face water. The relation of population to surface water is greater in Africa than anywhere else in the world. African land use by human populations is directed by the availability of water. Because of the scarcity of water, many areas are unfit places for human settlement. In tropical Africa's regions, dry plains are covered by a bare savanna with spiny shrubs. In contrast, the banks of rivers are covered with strips of dense, green vegetation which form gallery forests.

The Congo River is another important African river. Unlike the Nile and the Niger, its waters do not swell annually. Its 2,678-mile (4,320 km) course forms an arc that lies on both sides of the equator. The Congo River flows from east to west. It gathers water from many tributaries over a vast basin of 1,424,700 sq. miles (3,690,000 sq. km). The amount of its flow is second only to that of the Amazon River in South America. The Congo River crosses 2,852 miles (4,600 km) of equatorial forest. Its main tributary is the Lualaba River, which originates in the southeastern part of Zaire. When the English explorer Stanley explored the area around Lake Tanganyika, he followed the branch of the Congo that flows out of Lake Tanganyika.

Because the flow of the Congo River is constant, it flows without low and high seasons. In the spring, the small amount of water added by the northern tributaries is compensated for by the higher flow of southern tributaries. The opposite occurs in the fall. During this period, rains falling on the northern savannahs raise the water levels of northern tributaries.

Like other large African rivers, the Congo flows over unusual rock formations created long ago during Africa's geologic past. African *reliefs,* or elevations, are characterized by table-like rock formations. These originated partly from movements of the earth's crust and partly from erosion. They give the appearance of large tables situated at different heights. Rivers that flow over these tablelands form waterfalls, some of which are spectacularly beautiful. However, they prevent boats from passing.

There are about forty waterfalls along the course of the Congo River. The longest section of the river that can be navigated is about 932 miles (1500 km) long. It is located upstream from the Livingstone Cataracts. In this area, the two branches of the Congo reach a width of about 9 miles (14 km). They form two permanent shallow lakes, Lake Leopold II and Lake Tumba.

The foremost African river south of the equator is the

At various heights along the sides of the Rift Valley, a variety of different environments are inhabited by particular animals. Dense forests along the sides are home for small tree monkeys and small species of antelope. Plateaus and grasslands of the low plains are home for the largest species of mammals. Large lakes at the center of the Rift Valley are occupied by a rich community of aquatic animals.

Zambesi River. It originates in the mountains of Angola and southeastern Zaire and empties into the Indian Ocean. The Zambesi crosses 1,653 miles (2,660 km) of savannah in a region called "miombo." Within the miombo region, the land and the climate are similar to those of northern savannahs. However, the savannah in the Zambesi River basin is wilder than northern savannahs. The rains that fall from November to March turn the miombo into a marshy expanse. People cannot live in this wetland environment, but it is an ideal home for the aquatic birds and hoofed animals that dwell there. Because of its sandy soil, the region dries out almost completely during the dry season.

The most spectacular feature along the Zambesi River is Victoria Falls. This is the largest waterfall in Africa. At Victoria Falls, waters of the Zambesi River fall 393 feet (120 meters) through a crack in volcanic rock that is nearly 1 mile (1.5 km) wide.

The Great Fracture

Except for Lake Chad, Africa's major lakes are found in the eastern part of the continent. They are all located in a long, thin depression called a "rift." The rift extends from the

The calm waters of Lake Naivasha are shown. Almost 2,800 years ago, this lake was 131 feet (40 m) higher than at present. A high level of evaporation results in a concentrated salt content in these waters. In spite of this, large numbers of fish are able to survive in the lake.

Red Sea to the Mozambique Channel. It is only the African part of a series of cracks in the earth's crust. The rift begins in the lowest spurs of the Taurus Mountains in Turkey. It forms the Jordan River Valley, the Dead Sea, and the Red Sea. On the floor of the Dead Sea, the rift forms the lowest area of land on earth. Water covers the rift at the Dead Sea. Yet, the surface of the water is about 1,312 feet (400 m) below sea level.

Lake Victoria is Africa's largest lake. Part of its shoreline was formed by the edges of two main depressions in the area. Consequently, it receives a great amount of water from the streams of two different mountain chains. The lake has an area of over 26,255 sq. miles (68,000 sq. km). Its abundant supply of water provides a constant flow into the Nile River. Before reaching the Nile, the waters of Lake Victoria flow into Lake Albert.

A great variety of landscapes is found along the entire length of the Rift Valley, including deserts, grasslands, scrubs, and forests.

The East African Subplate

The great Rift Valley is a unique geological formation. Its existence and structure demonstrate a theory proposed seventy-five years ago by German scientist Alfred Wegener. Wegener's theory of continental drift suggests that the continents on the earth's crust drift and change location across time.

To observers, the enormous rock blocks that constitute the continental platforms, or plates, appear to be motionless. In reality, continental plates float on top of the heavier molten rock of the earth's upper mantle. The mantle separates the crust from the earth's core. The continents are

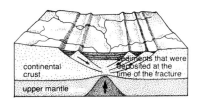

continental
crust

sediments that were
deposited at the
time of the fracture

upper mantle

The theory of "plate tectonics," or the movement of plates of the earth's crust, explains the drifting of continents. When two plates of crust move away from each other, the crust lying between them fractures and falls downward in blocks. In this way, a series of enormous parallel steps is formed (see diagram). This is how the Rift Valley in Africa was formed. As the separation of the plates continues, the fracture is filled with seawater. The seawater deposits sediments of minerals on top of the steps, so they are no longer visible. Molten rock from the upper mantle rises up in the center of the fracture as the fracture expands. The rising of molten rock causes volcanic activity.

blocks of crust that float and move on top of the fluid mantle. Earthquakes provide evidence of such crustal movements. But the speed of continental movement is very slow. It cannot be perceived by human senses or by scientific instruments. At most, the movement is little more than one inch per year. Movements correspond to the earth's rotational forces. These forces also determine the direction of winds and ocean currents.

The earth's crust is made up of about twenty blocks, or plates. About 200 million years ago, these plates were all united in one large supercontinent which scientists call "Pangaea." This supercontinent fragmented into smaller continents. Over time, the continents drifted apart. Today, it is possible to picture the outlines of the continents and see how they once fit together as one. Today, rock formations of plates that were located next to each other in the supercontinent have many similarities. For example, rock formations are similar in form and age at the edges of continents that once faced each other. Ancient mountain chains at the edge of one continent correspond to mountains at the edge of another continent. Plants and animals are similar in the areas where continents were joined. Differences between formerly connected continent margins are great where separation occurred early.

Pangaea began to break apart about 200 million years ago. The break began with the separation of the Antarctic plate block from the plate containing Africa. Later, India broke off from the African plate. The Himalayan Mountains formed when the Indian plate hit the Asian plate. The Madagascar plate broke off following this collision.

Today, breaking and moving events continue to shape the east African subplate. The western edge of this plate is the Rift Valley. The eastern edge is the Indian Ocean and the Mozambique Channel. The plate is not fragmenting in a rapid and distinct manner. Rather, it is undergoing a stretching and thinning process that takes millions of years. This affects all the rock layers in the outer crust of the continental block.

The outer crust is called the lithosphere. It extends from the surface to a depth of 48 miles (80 km). The lithosphere is fragile. Continuous forces of tension can easily fracture it. As blocks of crust slide, they form steps, various types of slopes, and depressions. Such formations appear along the walls of the African Rift Valley.

As the crust in this area is stretched, it becomes thinner.

Lake Logipi, in Kenya, provides evidence of volcanic activity in the Rift Valley region. Such activity results in highly-mineralized groundwater. Lake Logipi is an alkaline lake because its water contains large amounts of dissolved mineral salts.

New rock material is added to the area in the form of molten rock that comes from the upper mantle. Movements of molten rock cause volcanic activities. Sometimes these movements are considerable, resulting in the formation of very high volcanoes. This is the case with the volcanoes of the Virunga Mountains. They are situated in a cross fault, or a cross fracture, of the Rift Valley. The highest of these volcanoes has an elevation of 14,764 feet (4,500 m).

Underground water gushes out of hot springs near lakes that have permeable bottoms (bottoms that permit the seepage of water). This water contains a high concentration of minerals. It gushes out after contacting the upper layers of the mantle. This phenomenon is another demonstration of the thinness of the crust in this region.

Sixty-five million years ago, the island of Madagascar separated from the African plate. Fifteen million years ago, the sinking faults which created the Rift Valley became active. Within fifty million years, scientists think the east African subplate will be completely separated from the rest of Africa.

23

THE HIGHEST AFRICAN MOUNTAINS

The African continent is known for the vast arid areas of the Sahara Desert and large lakes of its eastern regions. It is also known for the tall peaks of Mount Kenya and Mount Kilimanjaro. Finally, it is known for the Ethiopian plateau, the largest rock mass of Africa.

Mount Kenya

Mount Kenya has an elevation of 17,060 feet (5,200 m). It is one of the highest peaks of Africa and is second only to Mount Kilimanjaro. This extinct and highly-eroded volcano is called "white mountain" in the language of the Kikuyu, the most numerous tribe of Kenya. This name comes from its white peak which is covered all year by glaciers. During the last glacial period, glaciers descended to an elevation of about 9,840 feet (3,000 m). Today, they are found beginning at an elevation of 14,765 feet (4,500 m). At the end of the nineteenth century, these glaciers began to move. Like all other glaciers of the world, they began to gradually retreat.

Mount Kenya can be divided into a series of fairly horizontal zones. These zones feature different types of vegetation. Between the elevations of 6,890 and 7,874 feet (2,100 and 2,400 m), Mount Kenya's slopes feature mountain forest vegetation. In areas between 7,874 and 9,186 feet (2,400 and 2,800 m) in elevation, bamboo trees grow well. In the zone ranging between 9,186 and 9,843 feet (2,800 and 3,000 m), most plants are of the *Hagenia* and *Hypericum* genera. Between 9,843 and 10,827 feet (3,000 and 3,300 m), moor, or marsh, vegetation grows. The alpine, or high mountain, zone extends from 10,827 to 14,108 feet (3,300 to 4,300 m). Above the alpine zone is a region of bare rock and glaciers.

Mount Kenya's forest vegetation zone features various types of plants. Compared to other zones, the greatest number of plant species is concentrated here. The camphor tree grows along the southeastern slopes. This native tree reaches a height of 147 feet (45 m). Lumber cut from its trunk is highly valued. Here large shrubs with fragrant flowers that belong to the madder family (Rubiaceae) grow. Ferns and plants of the touch-me-not family, such as the scarlet-flowered *Impatiens fischeri*, are also found here. Climbing plants such as *Begonia meyeri-johannis* and tree ferns 20 feet tall (6 m) grow in this zone.

Eastern African junipers and podocarp trees are the predominant plants along the dry western slopes. Common

Opposite page: High-elevation vegetation on Mount Kenya is dominated by giant senecios. The mountains, where the large rivers begin, have a tremendous variety of plants. Equatorial forests grow on low slopes. They are replaced by different plant communities at higher elevations. The zone of plant life near mountaintops is composed of tundra plants. Above this zone, there are only bare rocks and glaciers.

The height and the composition of the forests on Mount Kenya's slopes change according to elevation and exposure to the sun. Forest height ranges from bamboo thickets which are 10 feet (3 m) tall to impressive cedar forests that are 164 feet (50 m) tall. The mountain forest can be divided into three main zones. These are the rain forest, the bamboo forest, and the high-elevation forest.

trees also include the African olive and the *Classipourea malosana*. The *Classipourea malosana* has a columnar trunk that grows to a height of 59 feet (18 m). Ground cover is dense. A variety of plants which are green, not woody, grow here. They include violets, vetches, clover, and mint.

In the southwestern region of the mountain forest, the dragon tree is common. This slender tree reaches a height of 30 feet (9 m). It has thin branches that hang downward and leaves that are up to 12 inches (30 cm) long.

The rain forest includes many beautiful mosses, ferns, lichens, and orchids. At higher elevations, the "cloud forest" features gray and green lichens that hang like beards from tree branches. These growths create a mysterious and fascinating atmosphere. Clearings in the mountain forest are covered by the "Kikuyu grass." At the same elevation on the southeast side of Mount Kenya, a bamboo forest grows to heights of 50 feet (15 m).

The zone dominated by plants of the *Hagenia* and *Hypericum* genera features a forest cover of giant lobelias. During the flowering season, these plants grow to a height of 32 feet (10 m). Although the giant lobelia is shaped like a tree, it is actually a huge herb-like plant. Its flowers range in color from violet-red to blue. They are arranged in clusters

giant lobelia

senecio

The various species of giant lobelia and senecios are some of the most interesting plants of the African mountains. The large flower clusters of the giant lobelia are frequently visited by sunbirds looking for insects.

up to 6 feet (1.8 m) long. These clusters are similar to flower spikes and are hidden by *bracts*. Bracts are thread-like plant parts located below a flower or on the stalk of a flower cluster. Giant lobelias normally grow in groups in high mountains throughout eastern Africa. Within this zone, ground cover includes elderberry shrubs and plants of the lily and touch-me-not families.

Above the tree line, where trees are no longer found, a type of moor vegetation grows. This environment is an open marsh. The most characteristic plants of this zone are of the heath family. The tree heath is the most spectacular plant of this family. It grows to a height of 16 to 20 feet (5 to 6 m). Its small bell-shaped flowers are arranged in clusters. Over time, the colors of these flowers slowly change from white to pale violet to brown. Other common plants include clover, sedges, buttercups, and *Euryops brownei*. The latter is a shrub with yellow flowers. It reaches a height of 1.5 feet (0.5 m) and belongs to the family Compositae.

Two of the most striking plants of the alpine zone are the Kenyan lobelia and the senecio. The senecio reaches a height of 20 feet (6 m). Its flowers appear in large clusters and vary in color from maroon to yellow. This species is characteristic of the alpine zone of Mount Kenya, but it is also found in the Aberdare Mountain chain. During the flowering period, the Kenyan lobelia can reach a height of almost 6 feet (2 m). It grows exclusively in the alpine zone on Mount Kenya, at elevations of 9,842 feet (3,000 m) and above. Ground cover here consists of grasses and scattered flowering thistles. Throughout this zone, many areas are covered only by bare rock. Almost no vegetation is found at elevations above 14,108 feet (4,300 m). Only lichens are found growing in scattered areas.

The division of the mountains into different vegetational zones is also useful for studying animal distribution. The mountain forest, for example, is an ideal environment for many animals. Guenon monkeys, baboons, and duiker antelope are widespread. The forest is also home to buffalo and bushbuck antelope. Occasionally, elephants live here. Today, the northern and eastern areas are still inhabited by isolated black rhinoceroses. But this species is seriously threatened by extinction because of poaching and changes in the environment.

In the lower elevations of the mountain forest, defassa waterbucks live. Zebras inhabit the plain. Common elands, which are antelope, often graze on the grasses in forest

Several of the most typical animals of Mount Kenya are *(from left to right)*: defassa waterbuck, tree hyrax, Verreaux's eagle, serval, African civet, purple starling, and crested rat.

clearings and marshy zones. These hoofed animals are found at elevations up to 13,780 feet (4,200 m). The bongo also lives here but is seldom seen by visitors. This large, wary antelope is nocturnal, so it is active at night. It has a very keen sense of hearing. Bongos either live in pairs or in groups of up to thirty-five animals. Adult males live alone. Bongos feed on leaves and shoots of shrubs and vines, as well as rotting wood and bark. They are able to raise themselves up on their hind legs to browse on the tender leaves of trees.

The largest predator of the forest is the leopard. It is extremely difficult to find because it is active only at night.

Besides the bongo and the leopard, many other animals who are mainly nocturnal live here. Bats spend the day among the young leaves of banana trees and come out at night to hunt insects. Small antelope of the forest run through forest undergrowth at night.

Smaller nocturnal predators include the African civet, the serval cat, and the zorille, which is also called the African polecat. Large *herbivores*, or plant-eating animals, take advantage of the darkness to remain hidden from sight.

Nocturnal *omnivores*, which are animals that eat both plants and animals, also move about at night. These omnivores include the African porcupine and the forest hog. The African porcupine is the largest and heaviest rodent in Africa. The forest hog is a type of wild boar.

At elevations up to 14,764 feet (4,500 m), there are many subspecies of tree hyraxes, which are small, hoofed mammals. These subspecies are hard to tell apart. Rodents, such as the crested rat, live in dens dug into the soil of the dense forest. Although this rat lives on the ground, it can easily climb trees. This talent is due to its opposable thumbs. This means the thumb can be placed against the fingers and used to grasp trees and branches for climbing. In the mountains, African dormice are commonly found in cabins. They resemble the dormice that inhabit the forests of the Alps in Europe. Little is known of the habits of the African dormice.

At higher elevations, fewer species of plants and animals are found. In areas between the forest and moor zones, spotted hyenas, genets, mongooses, and porcupines live. At elevations between 10,827 and 14,108 feet (3,300 and 4,300 m) in the alpine zone, a species of hyrax is found. Hyraxes

A characteristic profile of Mount Kilimanjaro is seen from the savannah that encircles it.

Volcanic rock on the inside of Rim Crater on Mount Kilimanjaro is covered by this glacier. This is one of the closest glaciers to the equator.

live among the rocks in colonies of about sixty animals. Their habits are similar to those of groundhogs.

The highest elevations of the mountain forest and the neighboring open moor are homes for many birds of prey. These include the Verreaux's eagle, the Ruppell's vulture, the tufted eagle, and several types of buzzards. The smallest bird of prey living in this zone is the African sparrow hawk. The largest bird of prey here is the extremely rare crowned eagle. This bird hunts young antelope, pigs, and monkeys. Colobus monkeys are its main food source.

Within this zone, blue-crested touracos with bright red wing feathers are easily spotted in the green forest vege-

tation. These birds are called plantain-eaters because they eat the fruit of the plantain tree. Other brightly-colored birds live here, too. They include the purple starling, the black-headed oriole, and the multicolored sunbirds. Sunbirds feed on the nectar of flowers as well as on the insects that are found near the flowers.

Black African ducks and mountain wagtails inhabit areas near streams and rivers. The giant kingfisher is also found in these areas, although it is less common. It feeds mainly on freshwater crayfish.

The wattled ibis is another bird found in this region. Large flocks of this species move between feeding areas in grasslands and the areas where they roost for the night. These wading birds also live in the mountains of Aberdare and Usambara in Kenya and on Mount Kilimanjaro. In these areas, their characteristic call can frequently be heard in the distance. This call is also mixed with sounds made by multicolored Jardine's parrots. As night falls, calls of the bamboo francolin, or partridge, also fill the air.

Mount Kilimanjaro

Mount Kilimanjaro rises above the plateau of the lake country of eastern Africa. It extends above clouds which blanket elevations between 5,905 and 9,843 feet (1,800 to 3,000 m). The mountain's impressive mass originated from volcanic activity. It is formed by three ancient volcano craters. The largest volcanic crag, a steep, rugged cliff called Kibo, stands in the middle of the trio. It is covered by ice. Its peak, called Uhuru, has an elevation of 19,314 feet (5,887 m), making it the highest peak in Africa. To the east, the crag of the Mawenzi Volcano rises to an elevation of 16,892 feet (5,148 m). To the west, the highly-eroded Shira Volcano rises to an altitude of 13,133 feet (4,003 m).

The glaciers of Mount Kilimanjaro are slowly retreating like those of Mount Kenya and Mount Ruwenzori. In 1889, the Kibo Volcano was still covered by a compact ice cap. Its crater, which has a diameter of 1.55 miles (2.5 km), was filled by a gigantic mass of ice. Today, the eastern edge of the crater and the northern and eastern slopes of Kibo are almost completely free of ice and snow. The Weruweru is the largest stream of Kibo. It is fed by the meltwater of the Barranco Glacier. The meltwater of other glaciers enters small openings in the lava rock and emerges further down in the valley as spring-fed streams.

Mount Kilimanjaro features several terraces (leveled

Abbot's duiker

colobus monkey

African palm civet

African mole-rat

plains with a steep front) formed during past volcanic eruptions. These terraces formed from the solidification, or hardening, of the various sheets of lava flow.

As on Mount Kenya, the vegetation of Mount Kilimanjaro can be divided into zones, according to elevation. Each zone is characterized by dominant plants. Unlike Mount Kenya, Mount Kilimanjaro lacks a bamboo zone.

Between 6,234 and 9,843 feet (1,900 to 3,000 m) of elevation, Mount Kilimanjaro is almost completely surrounded by a rain forest. This strip of rain forest is very thin on the northwestern and northeastern sides. Several species of broadleaf trees grow here. They include the camphor tree, the Kilimanjaro olive, and several species of figs and spurges.

In the rain forest, tree trunks are covered by mosses and lichens. Long ribbons of mosses and filmy ferns hang down from tree branches. A great number of plants such as clubmosses, docks, wormwoods, bitter cress, and violets grow on the ground.

Conifer trees such as podocarps and East African junipers grow on Kilimanjaro's upper slopes. Precipitation is rather scarce along these slopes.

As its name suggests, the cloud forest is always covered by clouds. Vegetation here is extremely luxuriant. Like the cloud forest of Mount Kenya, trees of this forest have beards of pale green lichens hanging from their branches. *Hagenia abyssinica* grows in the higher areas of the cloud forest.

The moor zone is above the cloud forest. Heath plants in the lower part of the moor reach a height of 30 feet (9 m). However, these plants become shorter and shorter as the elevation increases. Other than the heath, the most common plants of the moor are *Philippa excelsa* and *Senecio kilimanjari*. Both of these plants grow in humid areas. The ground is covered by fescue grasses as well as the yellow flowers and the red and silver flowers of two species of the *Helichrysum* genus. Occasionally, isolated flowering plants of gladiolus, anemones, geraniums, lilies, and orchids grow here. A native species of lobelia stands out among the many flowers. This ancient species reaches a height of up to 6 feet (2 m).

The giant senecio grows in the alpine zone. This plant grows very slowly. It reaches the age of flowering and a height of 23 feet (7 m) after about two hundred years.

Mount Kilimanjaro's coldest vegetation band begins at an elevation of 14,108 feet (4,300 m). There is not much

Opposite page: Pictured are some typical animals of Mount Kilimanjaro.

Right: The small and graceful Zanzibar antelope is among the most timid of animals. It is, therefore, difficult to observe. It is active mostly at night or in the early hours of the morning. It takes shelter in forests and shrub thickets growing on mountain slopes.

growth of green plants in this area. Dominant plants are grasses and various species of the *Helichrysum* genus.

No seed-bearing plants can survive above an elevation of 16,077 feet (4,900 m). The only plants found at this altitude are several isolated ferns and mosses. These can even be found growing on the high peak of Kibo Volcano.

The mountain forest of Kilimanjaro is inhabited by the same animal species that are found on Mount Kenya. To avoid repetition, mention will be made only of the most characteristic species. One such animal is the elephant. The open forest of the northwestern side of Kilimanjaro is the preferred environment of elephants. However, these animals also live at higher elevations.

Trees of the mountain forest are ideal homes for colobus monkeys. These graceful black and white monkeys were on the verge of extinction at the end of the last century. Their long fur was prized in Europe as a luxury item. In 1882 alone, 175,000 of these furs were sold on the European market. The monkey was saved from extinction when styles for furs changed to other animal species.

Dense underbrush of the mountain forest is inhabited by forest antelope. The Natal duiker antelope has a reddish

chestnut coat of hair and curved horns. Several subspecies of the Natal duiker are distinguished by the color of their coats. One subspecies lives in the area between Mount Kilimanjaro and the Juba River. Another subspecies, the Abbot's duiker, inhabits the mountain forest of Mount Kilimanjaro. This is one of the few environments that is suitable to the needs of this animal. Abbot's duiker lives at elevations of up to 8,858 feet (2,700 m).

The Zanzibar antelope also prefers a dense underbrush of shrubs and tree trunks. This animal has two large glands in the snout that produce a liquid with a strong musk odor. The habitat of the Zanzibar antelope also extends to an elevation of 8,858 feet (2,700 m).

In the natural environment of Kilimanjaro, visitors can often find tracks and feces of leopards. However, it is extremely difficult for visitors to see this wary nocturnal predator. But the leopard is not the only predator here. Like Mount Kenya, the mountain forest of Mount Kilimanjaro is also inhabited by small predators. These include zorilles, genets, African civets, African palm civets, and African wild cats.

The zorille is one of the many weasel-like animals that inhabit the mountain forests of Africa.

37

Rock formations on the Ethiopian plateau are ancient and are divided by the African Rift. The plateau is a large volcanic tableland. It rose upward when the bordering area dropped. This occurred between 36 and 58 million years ago, during the Eocene epoch. Presently, ancient volcanoes rise above the tableland. In the past, there were many more bodies of water on the plateau than there are today. Today, the plateau is relatively dry. But its precipitation is still the main water source for the Blue Nile and its precious load of silt.

Neither bongos nor forest hogs are found in the forests of Mount Kilimanjaro, though they inhabit those of Mount Kenya. The large expanse of the savannah separating these two mountains has prevented their spread to Kilimanjaro forests.

The gray duiker is found in areas up to the snow line. This species is the only antelope of the area that has colonized open environments. It inhabits an area extending from the edges of the desert to the peaks of the highest mountains. It feeds mainly on plant material such as leaves, twigs, shoots, bark, and fruit. However, stomach contents of several gray duikers indicate that they also eat animals such as insects and chicks of guinea hens.

The moor and the alpine zone are inhabited by a small number of animal species. The most significant of these are numerous species of rodents. These include the African mole-rat and the striped field mouse. The striped field mouse is found at elevations of up to 13,124 feet (4,000 m). It builds its nest in the open, on the ground, and in underground dens. This little rodent eats mainly grasses and seems to be social. Families of thirty mice have been found in a single den. The larger mammals of these two zones include the klipspringer antelope and the black-fronted duiker. The only mammals that are found above 15,092 feet (4,600 m) are a few swamp rats.

Many birds live in the shrubby moor and in alpine meadows where bushes of the *Protea* genus grow. Various species of sunbirds are attracted to the yellow flowers of the bushes of the *Leonitis* genus and to the torch lily flowers. Sunbirds, including the emerald-tailed species, eat nectar produced by these flowers. Other birds, such as Shelley's francolin and the stonechat, also prefer the moor. Unlike the European stonechat, the African species does not migrate during the winter.

The white-necked crow nests among rocks. It measures 22 inches (55 cm). This crow is completely black except for a white, half-moon spot on the back of the neck. It also nests lower in the valley where it feeds on garbage and food scraps found near human settlements.

The Ethiopian Plateau

The eastern African Rift, or crack, divides Ethiopia into two parts. These are the Ethiopian plateau to the west and the Somalian plateau to the southeast.

Because it is hard to reach, the Ethiopian plateau

The vervet monkey is able to live in a variety of environmental conditions. It is one of the least-demanding animals of the Ethiopian plateau's forests. It is common in small wooded areas in southern parts of the plateau.

represents a sort of natural fortress. It is bordered by high mountains to the northwest. The plateau plunges 6,562 to 9,842 feet (2,000 to 3,000 m) to the northeast. It also plunges 3,281 to 4,921 feet (1,000 to 1,500 m) to the southeast. The plateau can be reached from the southwest and west by crossing deep valleys.

About seventy million years ago, this region was covered by the sea. Minerals that were deposited on the bottom of that sea hardened into rock formations. Today, these formations are called "sedimentary rocks." In Ethiopia, there are vast formations of these sedimentary rocks. They are composed of sandstone, limestone, and gypsum, depending on the different types of minerals that they contain.

Between thirty-six and fifty-eight million years ago, this area was changed by extensive volcanic activity. Enormous rivers of lava flowed one on top of the other. In several zones, the layer of solidified lava rock is 6,562 feet (2,000 m) thick. This layer covers a lower rock layer. Today, some similar changes in rock layers of the area are still occurring. In addition, continuous movements of the earth's crust cause earthquakes, volcanic activity, and hot springs.

The eastern part of the Ethiopian plateau lies 9,842 feet (3,000 m) above sea level. The northwestern part exceeds an elevation of 13,123 feet (4,000 m). The highest peak of Ethiopia, Ras Dashan, is located in this area. It reaches an elevation of 15,158 feet (4,620 m).

The Ethiopian plateau is crossed by deep gorges in which fast rivers flow during the rainy period. The Abbai River originates 4,921 feet (1,500 m) below Lake Tana. It crosses layers of volcanic rock, limestone, and sandstone in Ethiopia. It becomes the upper course of the Blue Nile. The valley of the Abbai River is 18 miles (30 km) wide and is almost always covered by fog. It vaguely resembles the Grand Canyon in Arizona.

The Ethiopian plateau can be divided into four zones. The lowest, called "Kolla," reaches an elevation of 5,905 feet (1,800 m). The next highest, the "Woina Dega," has elevations of 5,905 to 8,202 feet (1,800 to 2,500 m). These are followed by the "Dega" at 8,202 to 11,483 feet (2,500 to 3,500 m) and the "alpine zone" above 11,483 feet (3,500 m).

THE MARSHES OF THE SUDD REGION

The flood plains have long been among the richest natural environments in Africa. Grassland zones of the Serengeti Plain and the Senegal savannahs are rich in animal inhabitants. However, these areas are only half as rich as the great marshes of Sudan. This marshy region is called "Sudd."

The Nile River Basin

In the southern part of Sudan, the Nile River is surrounded by vast low areas. These depressions extend over thousands of square miles. Rainwater and river water gather in these low areas, creating an endless series of marshes.

At these latitudes, there is a short dry season followed by long, abundant rains. In this region, the Nile River has a large and relatively constant flow. Water flows into marshes and collects there because of the rolling terrain.

All of these factors contribute to create permanent surface water. This water is rapidly invaded by particular types of plants that can be found only in this part of Africa. For example, the rigid stems of papyrus plants and water cabbages grow in this territory. They also grow in marshy Uganda.

The marshy areas of Uganda occupy about 4,633 sq. miles (12,000 sq. km). These marshes are extensively covered with papyrus plants. Coverage is so thick that very little light filters through to the water below. Consequently, there are very few plants, except for sphagnum mosses, in the undergrowth. These plants prefer the acidic environment created by marsh conditions.

The largest wetland areas are near the Nile River. A large 124-mile (200 km) wide marsh surrounds the Victoria Nile in the area between Lake Victoria and Lake Kyoga. Farther north, the Nile flows into a small valley that ends with the Murchison Falls. This is the northern part of the Rift Valley. Beyond Lake Albert, the Nile is obstructed by a mountain chain. It widens out over a vast area of about 57,900 sq. miles (150,000 sq. km). There it forms a seemingly endless marsh region that is crossed by other rivers.

During flooding periods, this region is completely under water. During dry periods, the region is carpeted with plants, including cockspur-grasses, cattails, and certain grasses. Temperatures are always high, and sunlight is intense. These factors contribute to extensive plant growth. During the year, the green carpet of plants on the water surface becomes rich and thick. Among these plants are

Opposite page: African elephants are the largest land animals in the world. Surprisingly enough, they find their most favorable environments in vast river floodplains and lakes. They prefer these environments because of the richness of the plant life. Other numerous animals found in these habitats are rhinoceroses, hippopotamuses, buffaloes, and various species of antelope.

water lilies, floating ferns, and water cabbages. In fact, this carpet of plants can become so thick that nonfloating plants are able to sprout and take root on them. Gradually, larger and larger plants are able to colonize, or grow on, this carpet.

The colonization process begins with the germination, or the sprouting, of grass seeds. It reaches its peak with the growth of several species of cyperus plants, such as the papyrus. Through this colonization, the mat of vegetation that covers the marsh becomes several feet thick. It can hold the weight of large antelopes that take shelter among papyrus plants. Large blocks of these floating mats are separated by arms, or canals, of nearly still water. In these canals, clumps of plants called "palm savannah" grow like islands. Two plants, *Hyphaene thebaica* and *Borassus aethiopica*, are commonly found in these clumps. There are also small islands of clay-like soil covered by an acacia savannah-type

Right: The Nile River receives water from the important lakes of the Rift Valley. Along its course, the river widens into vast marshy areas that are covered by a thick, aquatic vegetation. These areas are the preferred habitat of hippopotamuses and birds.

Marsh vegetation often includes floating plants like the "water cabbage." This plant is not related to the garden cabbage. During the dry season, water cabbages are partially rooted to the bottom of the marsh *(above)*. In periods of high water, they freely float on top of the water *(below)*. This is the first stage in the formation of floating mats of compact vegetation.

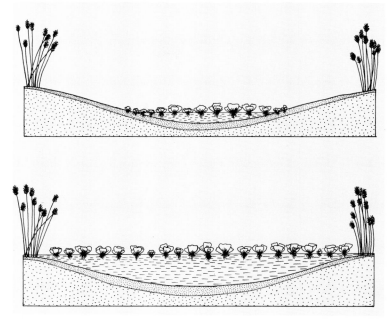

of vegetation. Semiaquatic plants which also grow near dry land often connect these floating "islands" to clumps of savannah. The most typical is the floating fern. This plant can withstand periods of partial dryness in the soil or in the material on which it grows.

During the highest floods, the large floating plant mats become detached from the land. They drift with the flow of the river. Some of the plants that are transported in this manner include bladderworts. These plants trap and eat aquatic insects that live in stagnant water. Sometimes several blocks of plants come together and create a sort of dam. This causes increased flooding in surrounding marshland.

Water on the bottom of the marshes contains very little oxygen. This results from the decaying of large amounts of plant matter, a process which consumes oxygen dissolved in water. Many species of tropical fish can survive in these waters because they evolved breathing systems which allow them to breathe oxygen from the air.

The Animals

These marshes are ideal environments for many species of aquatic birds. The shoebill stork is found only in the papyrus beds of the Sudd region, where it feeds on frogs and small fish.

The concentration of mammals in this region is also

A white rhinoceros stands out against the green background of a marsh. Marshes of the Sudd region along the left bank of the Nile River are important environments for the conservation of this species. In all of northern Africa, the white rhinoceros is found only in this region. Its distribution is similar to that of Sudan lechwes, a species of antelope.

amazing. The ideal environment for many of these mammals is not the marsh, but the fertile land that is exposed after marsh waters recede. But animals are adapted to moving about in marshes and on top of floating mats of vegetation.

These marsh areas have the largest total mass of plants and animals per square mile (or square kilometer) of the entire planet. This is due, in part, to the extremely high productivity of vegetation. It also results from the fact that many large animals live here, including buffalos, hippopotamuses, and elephants.

An adult elephant weighs an average of four tons. Its mass of bones and muscles is comparable to that of an entire herd of waterbuck antelope or gazelles. A hippopotamus weighs two to three tons. Two buffalo together weigh one ton. Only grasslands as rich as these can provide enough food to support populations of these giant animals.

These large animals are able to walk over soft marsh areas after emerging from the water. This is possible because of adaptations of their feet. In elephants, for example, five toes are united in a block of fatty and fibrous tissue. Together the toes form a wide, flat surface that distributes weight evenly. Because of this special adaptation, this huge animal is able to walk on unstable ground without sinking. An equivalent area of an elephant's foot exerts less pressure than the heel of a woman's shoe. But the toes of the elephant work independently. They are sensitive enough to enable this animal to walk on almost any type of ground surface.

In this environment, elephants eat mostly plants. They are able to destroy brushy undergrowths in short periods of time. White rhinoceroses eat the same kinds of plants that elephants eat. The rhinoceros's large upper lip is perfectly suited for browsing on vegetation.

Both white rhinoceroses and black rhinoceroses are found in the marshes of the Sudd region. This is one of the most important regions on earth for the conservation of these species. The white rhinoceros is the larger of the two. It is considerably less common than the black rhinoceros. Its range is limited to the area on the left bank of the Nile River. The Nile River acts as an uncrossable obstacle for the spreading of this species. Northern Uganda and the nearby region of Sudan represents the core of its distribution in northern Africa.

The black rhinoceros is more common in eastern Africa. Food and water are plentiful here, so a large number of black rhinoceroses live in this region. On the average, there is one rhinoceros for every 2.7 sq. miles (7 sq. km) in this area.

The variety of animal species in the Sudd is evident in the great abundance of antelope and goat species that live there. The smallest and most agile of these species are the gray duikers, the duikers, and the oribis. The largest are the bushbuck and nyala antelope. Their size is halfway between a buffalo and a gazelle. However, these antelope have slender bodies and long legs. Their backs are either straight or curved downward in the middle. They are identifiable by

long snouts that have less hair than those of other antelope.

The greater kudu is a huge antelope. It is 4 to 5 feet (1.2 to 1.5 m) tall at the shoulder and sometimes exceeds a length of 6 feet (2 m). It has powerful horns which are twisted in a spiral. These horns reach a maximum length of 5 feet (1.7 m). The kudu is distributed over a vast territory, extending from the savannahs of Chad to Ethiopia. From this northern limit, it spreads as far south as South Africa, although it is rare in that country. In the past, the greater kudu migrated within this region, following rain fronts. These migrations are not completely understood.

Various species of gazelles, zebras, and gnus migrate to the region of the Serengeti Plain. This region is as rich in plants and animals as the Sudd region.

Among the bushbucks, nyalas, and kudus, the sitatunga is the species that is best adapted to wetland areas. This antelope is relatively small. It is only two-thirds the size of the greater kudu. Its hooves are particularly long, and their surface area can be extended somewhat when the animal runs. This feature enables the animal to move easily over

Two male greater kudus stand alert. These antelope are identified by their typical spirally-curved horns. Horns of the male can reach a length of 5.5 feet (1.7 m). The female is hornless. Generally, females live in herds with young males. Adult males join these groups only during the mating season. The rest of the time they live either alone or in small groups. These groups may only include two or three animals.

48

Migration routes of plant-eating animals within the Serengeti National Park are shown with red arrows. Large migrations of antelope, gnus, and zebras take place in this park and in the eastern zone of the Rift Valley. Movements of animals are determined by the availability of water and the arrival of the rainy season.

slippery mud. The sitatunga is also an excellent swimmer. In case of immediate danger, it jumps into the water. With only its nostrils sticking out of the water, it swims away. The animal's association with marshes is even more evident from its diet. Its diet consists of shoots and leaves of papyrus plants as well as other aquatic plants.

The Water Antelope

Besides the sitatunga, there are several other species of antelope that could be considered "aquatic." These are reedbucks, waterbucks, and lechwe antelope.

Waterbucks are distributed throughout the African continent. They include thirteen subspecies. The waterbucks are large animals, often weighing over 441 pounds (200 kilograms). Their tails are long, almost reaching the heel. Long hair covers their bodies, forming drooping bunches. Longer hair on their necks forms a sort of mane. The subspecies that lives in the Sudd region is characterized by a white spot on the rump.

Among the species of reedbucks, waterbucks, and lechwes found here, only males have horns. These horns consist of a series of horny rings similar in appearance to the horns of the European wild goat.

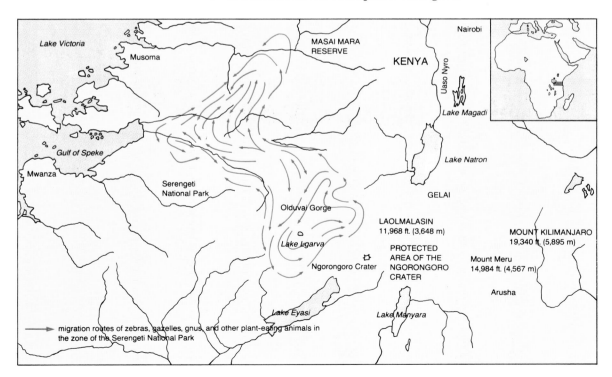

migration routes of zebras, gazelles, gnus, and other plant-eating animals in the zone of the Serengeti National Park

49

Horns of waterbucks rarely exceed 31 inches (80 centimeters) in length. They curve to the rear and then upward. They are more than just a simple ornament for these animals. They often are used by males during fights over territories or for the domination of females. During such fights, males face each other with threatening postures, showing off their horns. Then they begin to hit each other with blows to the head. They strongly push each other, or they lock horns and try to knock one another to the ground.

Waterbucks are territorial animals. They do not make true migrations but follow the changing water levels. The main part of a male's territory consists of the bank or shore of a body of water. This is usually in an area of reed beds where the animal can take shelter during periods of inactivity. It has been observed that the aggressiveness of males decreases when they are farther away from bushy, wetland

The kob is a slender antelope with rather unusual habits. This species has unique courtship habits that make it easy to observe.

areas. Females are never attacked because they are submissive. Mating does not occur during a distinct mating season. But most young are born during the dry season. In Uganda and Kenya, waterbucks graze in the open savannah during the day. Farther north, where temperatures are higher, they rest during daylight hours and are active at night.

Like sitatungas, waterbucks tend to seek refuge in the water in case of danger. Their coats of hair are waterproofed by a substance produced by their skin glands. However, waterbucks do not flee often. They appear to be fearless. This behavior makes them easy targets for hunters. The waterbuck's greatest protection against hunters is the disagreeable texture and taste of its meat. Since the beginning of the century, zoologists have known that the meat of this animal is of a poor quality and not fit for human consumption.

Pictured are male and female lechwes of Sudan. Males of this rare antelope species are a different color and size than females. Females do not have horns. When physical features of the male differ greatly from those of the female, the species is said to be "sexually dimorphic."

Kobs are very similar to waterbucks, but they are slightly smaller and have shorter and stockier horns. Kob antelope have short hair and lack manes. The Uganda kob has been the most studied subspecies of this animal. It is particularly known for its courtship behavior. The kob is the only hoofed animal whose males gather in courtship arenas during the mating period. Up to thirty or forty males gather in one small area near a river or stream. Here the males mark off their individual territories and then challenge each other. Their fights are rarely bloody or fatal. For the most part, they are ritual fights. These territorial fights are very frequent. The territories of males are very small. In fact, they are rarely more than 430 sq. yards (360 sq. m), and, because of this size, males often encounter each other.

Normally, females live in groups with young males. They only enter the courtship arena during *estrus*, which is a period of sexual excitement. When females enter the arena, the males become quite excited and exhibit the striped hair of their legs and the white spots under their chins. This is done by rearing up on the hind legs. At the peak of the excitement, the chosen male touches the female several times with its front legs. Then mating occurs.

Unlike all other hoofed animals, the male kob courts the female even after mating takes place. The male sniffs the female and then touches her with one leg. This is a gesture that animal species usually make only before mating.

Reedbucks live alone. They are wary and shy. Reedbucks are graceful animals that resemble roe deer in size and color. But the reedbucks are smaller and more slender.

The small-horned reedbuck lives in this part of Africa. It is distributed over a band of territory that extends from the Atlantic Ocean to the Indian Ocean. This particular reedbuck lives in pairs or small family groups. It lives in wooded areas near rivers and marshes. It often hides among the reed beds and tall grasses that grow in these environments. This species is easily recognized by its small horns, which are rarely longer than 12 inches (30 cm), and reddish coat of short, bristly hair. The hair is longer below the neck and on the underside of the body. Because of its shy nature, it is very difficult to view this animal. The small-horned reedbuck is very wary of humans because it is widely hunted by local people. In times of danger, the animal flees from marshy areas. It is less inclined to swim than other species of antelope.

The lechwe antelope prefers marshy environments

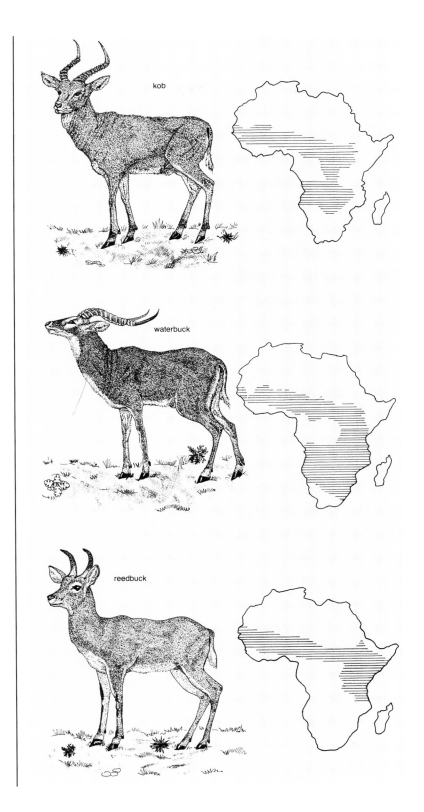

Kob, waterbuck, and reedbuck antelope are typical of the marshes of the Sudd region. In the drawing, they are shown next to their areas of distribution. The size of the area of distribution of many antelope is strictly dependent on the availability of water. Distribution areas are either the same or partially the same as distribution areas for floodplains.

A spotted hyena disturbs a group of
vultures. Part of the hyena's diet
includes animal carcasses. Hyenas are
usually unsocial. When necessary, they
gather in groups to hunt antelope in
open zones. Hunting in organized
groups is more efficient for capturing
larger prey.

Cultivated fields grow at the base of the inactive Ngorongoro Volcano. Volcanic soils are very fertile, but it is hard to use modern farming methods here. Primitive farming methods are highly conditioned by the arrival of the rainy season.

with tall plants. Of all the antelope, this species takes best advantage of food resources of marsh plants. Lechwes are able to move easily over the slipperiest ground of mud and wet mats of vegetation. This ability comes from their long hooves. While running, the weight of the animal is supported by the hoof and by the fetlock (the area just above the hoof). This increased supportive surface gives the animal greater stability when running.

No other species can run as easily as the lechwe over slippery surfaces. It is easy for it to flee from attacks by large wildcats. In case of extreme danger, lechwes make a running dive into the deepest water. There is less chance of

being attacked by a crocodile than by a cheetah or lion.

Lechwes enter marsh areas during periods of low water. During such periods, they form groups of up to fifty animals. During periods of high water, they scatter into dry land areas.

Males and females of this species have coats of different colors. In fact, their colors are so different that they may seem to belong to two different species. This feature is very rare among antelope. The adult males have a reddish-brown coat with a precise pattern of light spots on the backside. This pattern looks like a saddle with reins and is present only in males. Coats of females are a uniform pale yellow color. Males have long slender horns similar to those of kobs. Females do not have horns.

The lechwe is the most common antelope of the Sudd marshes. Antelope that are closely related to this species live in the distant savannahs of southern Africa. The survival of the lechwe is tied to the conservation of Africa's wetland environments. It is more dependent on wetland environments than the waterbuck, the elephant, or the white rhinoceros.

The Human Presence

The animals that live in this territory represent a valuable source of food for humans. Because of the animal population, several local ethnic groups developed social systems based on hunting. The Nuer, for example, live south of the Bahr el Arab River, which flows into the Nile. For centuries, these people hunted crocodiles, elephants, and hippopotamuses. Today, the Nuers dedicate themselves to raising rice and potato crops. The Bari live farther south. Originally they fished. Today, they raise goats and cultivate mango and banana trees.

Agriculture in these regions is an old practice. It was developed because of a decrease in the number of animals that could be hunted. The raising of plant crops is an alternative food production system that has been used in this area since ancient times. Long ago, black tribes of ancient Nubia converted wild areas to patches of cultivated plants. The Massakim, Kukulu, and Korongo tribes developed a primitive type of agriculture that produced cotton, millet, tobacco, and sesame. Fields of these crops were sometimes located miles away from villages. Survival of these tribes and villages required intensive work. Little time was left for leisure activities.

THE INHABITANTS OF LAKES AND RIVERS

The first important discoveries of fish species that live in the waters of Africa's interior were made by Eduard Rüppell and Etienne Geoffroy Saint-Hilaire. These zoologists conducted explorations along the Nile and in the region of the Red Sea.

Fish

In Africa, as in the other continents, almost all the freshwater fish belong to the large order Cypriniformes. In this order, the swim bladder, the sack of gas that keeps the fish balanced in the water, is directly connected to the throat cavity by a canal. This canal allows the fish to fill its swim bladder with air breathed in from the mouth at the water's surface. The complete swelling of the swim bladder can take over an hour. This connecting canal present in freshwater fish generally is absent in marine fish.

The most common African fish belong to the family of minnows and carps. Some minnows and carps are native to Africa. Others also are commonly found throughout Europe and Asia.

The cichlid family is almost as important and widespread as the minnow and carp family. Cichlids are typical tropical freshwater fish. Like barbs, cichlids do not have teeth on the jaw. Instead, their teeth are located in the throat, attached to a bone. In many instances, these teeth have different shapes. Some have the shape and function of mammal molars. Many species of cichlids feed primarily on plants. They have relatively wide, flat teeth that grind and chew plant material in a manner similar to that of cows.

The various species of cichlids have colonized almost all of the rivers and lakes on the continent. The exception to this case are mountain streams and caverns. However, various species of cave-dwelling barbs live in cavern waters. They are blind and have no color or scales. All of the surface waters of Africa are inhabited by at least one of the hundreds of species belonging to the cichlid family. There are even species that live at great depths in lakes such as Lake Tanganyika.

Cichlids are normally small in size. They live in shallow waters and are very important to the food supply. In their environments, they form the basis of a food chain that includes larger fish and predators such as crocodiles and humans. A surprising variety of cichlids lives in the lakes of the Rift Valley. Ninety species of cichlids live in Lake Tanganyika. Eighty-nine of these species are native. Of the 175

Opposite page: The black-and-white kingfisher is a common inhabitant of African riverbanks. This is only one of the many bird species that feed on fish found in waters of the African interior.

Carp live in a small lake in Ninzima Springs, Kenya. Many of the freshwater fish in Africa belong to the minnow and carp family. This family is the most widespread and has the largest number of species of all fish families in the continent. These fish are characterized by the presence of one or two pairs of whisker-like *barbels* on the upper jaw.

species found in Lake Nyasa, 171 are native. This extraordinary variety probably results from the large size and isolation of these lakes. Both factors aided the evolution of many species over a long period of time. Lake Albert, which was connected to the Nile basin for many years, contains only seven species of cichlids. Only two of them are native species.

There are other fish families worthy of note. These include spiny eels, labyrinth-fish, topminnows, and catfish. Labyrinth-fish are large fish with flattened bodies. They often are kept in aquariums. Egg-laying topminnows are

similar to carps and minnows but have jaw teeth. African freshwater bodies are inhabited by 250 species of catfish.

Nowhere else in the world is fish life as abundant as in Africa. Only tropical waters are able to sustain a high number of species having vegetarian diets. Microscopic algae and single-celled animal organisms called zooplankton float in African waters. They are very important to the food chain of these waters. They use phosphorus and nitrogen in the water and light energy from the sun to produce food. Tropical waters collect little *humus*, or decayed plant matter. Nutrients such as phosphorus and nitrogen produced by decaying plants circulate freely in the water. There these nutrients are recycled quickly into new plant structures. Fats and proteins from microscopic algae are the main foods for many small fish. These small fish are eaten, in turn, by larger fish.

Africa's periodic floods play an important role in aquatic environments. Floods increase the food supply for several fish species. During the rainy seasons, flood waters cover tropical plains and invade dense equatorial forests. As a result, plant-eating fish of the marshes are able to swim into new areas. There they eat large amounts of tender leaves which are covered by flood waters. As partially digested leaves are expelled by the fish, they fall to the bottom. There they are eaten by scavenger fish such as the *Tilapia*, a genus of cichlid.

African waters are rich because of abundant food resources and fertility resulting from floods. It is not by chance that the largest human settlements on the continent first arose near Africa's main lakes and rivers. The first of these settlements belonged to the Egyptian civilization. These settlements thrived in areas bordering the Nile River.

While exploring Lake Tanganyika with Livingstone, Stanley wrote in his journal that the shores of the Nile were like a garden of Eden for the tribes of the area. He wrote, "How easy life must be for these fishermen! The lake provides them with enough fish to live on, as well as an extra amount that they sell and trade for other goods. Their wives cultivate the slopes of the hills and harvest corn, cassava roots, peas, potatoes, and acorns. The palm fruits produce abundant amounts of food oil, and the plantain trees produce sweet fruit. They carve canoes out of giant tree trunks that they find in ravines and among the crumbly soil. Nature has abundantly furnished them with everything a man could desire for his material and emotional well-being."

The drawing on the left shows Lake Victoria. The drawing on the right shows an area of the lake called the "Gulf of Nyanza." Nile perch were introduced into the gulf in the mid-1960s. They soon began to spread and prey on small fish of the cichlid family. Today, almost all the gulf's small cichlids have been killed by Nile perch. Cichlids were once an important food source for local people.

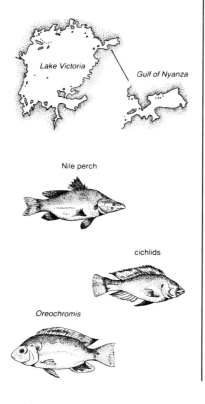

Lake Victoria

Gulf of Nyanza

Nile perch

cichlids

Oreochromis

This meeting with the fishermen occurred after an eight-month trip across deserts, swamps, and forests.

Reports from the explorers tell how fishing can be the source of food on a continent where conditions are largely unfavorable to humans. Fish represent a valuable source of protein. They can be easily caught with fishing tools such as nets. Fossil evidence shows that fish were used as a food source as early as the Paleolithic period, between 15,000 and 750,000 years ago.

In several areas of Africa, cichlids of the genus *Tilapia* were introduced into rice paddies. This was done to increase the protein supply for African people. These fish multiply very fast. They feed mainly on unused parts of rice plants. Thus, they produce large amounts of high-protein food at very low cost.

An Incautious Program

Fish are often moved from one location to another. This is done to increase the production of food for human populations. However, such efforts often are successful only when conditions can be strictly controlled. The introduction of fish into a new location can work against efficiency of food production. This happened in Lake Victoria.

Lake Victoria has an area of 26,500 sq. miles (68,635 sq. km). Its waters are inhabited by one of the largest and most varied fish populations on the continent. An important local economy is based on the catching of small cichlids which are plant-eaters or scavengers. These fish are at the base of the food pyramid. Harvesting these fish is efficient from a food production standpoint. These fish eat plants or organic debris, grow, and are harvested by humans. They are not part of a food chain involving intermediate steps where larger fish feed on smaller fish and humans eventually feed on the larger fish. Within such food chains, seventy to ninety percent of the fish mass is lost at each intermediate step. It takes about 22 pounds (10 kg) of small fish to feed a 2-pound (1 kg) predator fish.

Where fish serve as a major food source, many factors determine how many fish can be caught. The danger of overfishing is a cause for worry. In spite of this knowledge, the Nile perch was introduced into Lake Victoria during the 1960s. The Nile perch, which reaches a weight of 198 pounds (90 kg), is one of the most savage of all the African predator fish. It was not long before this predator began to work against the efficiency of food production.

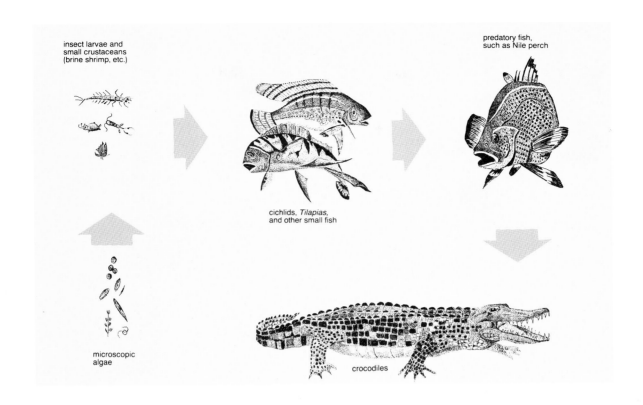

insect larvae and
small crustaceans
(brine shrimp, etc.)

predatory fish,
such as Nile perch

cichlids, *Tilapias*,
and other small fish

microscopic
algae

crocodiles

This drawing shows a typical food chain of the river and lake environments. In these environments, microscopic algae, known as *phytoplankton*, play a magic role. Phytoplankton is eaten by microscopic animal organisms, *zooplankton*, and by specialized forms of larger animals. The food chain is more complex than it appears here. Eggs and the fry of the same fish can occupy different positions in the food chain at various times.

Nile perch spread rapidly in the northern part of the lake. They reached the waters of Kenya in less than five years. Next, they invaded the waters of Tanzania. This spread of the Nile perch led to a series of unforeseen consequences. For example, schools of a native cichlid (*Oreochromis esculentus*) were widely preyed upon by the Nile perch. As a result, this cichlid practically disappeared from the Gulf of Nyanza. Before introduction of perch, native cichlids supplied food to the area around Nairobi, Kenya's capital, and nearby cities. Records of fish catches during the 1960s show that 80 percent of the total weight of the fish taken from this gulf was Nile perch. Eventually, the number of smaller fish was not great enough to feed the large population of predatory Nile perch. The population of Nile perch began to make rapid changes because of its unbalanced population.

When Nile perch first were introduced, they began to feed on small species of cichlids such as those of the genus *Oreochromis*. After practically eliminating this resource, they began to feed on shrimp. Shrimp make up a large part of the diet for fish that are up to 3 feet (1 m) long.

Stagnant water is almost always covered by a layer of vegetation. Water lilies, such as the river cabbage, represent the first stage of the formation of floating mats of vegetation.

The introduction of the Nile perch upset the natural balance of fish communities in many African aquatic environments. In addition, the introduction upset local economies. The meat of the Nile perch was not appreciated by local people. It sold for thirty times less than the small fish that originally inhabited the lake.

Because of its large body size and fatty nature, meat from the Nile perch cannot be dried in the sun. The meat must be smoked in order to preserve it. This necessity led to another environmental problem, the cutting of forests on numerous islands. The cutting was done to obtain the wood necessary to smoke the perch. In addition, large, expensive nets are required to capture Nile perch. Many small fishing companies could not afford these nets. This combination of factors gradually created a monopoly in Africa's fishing industry. Presently, only a few rich producers control the entire market for this product.

In 1984, the United Nation's Food and Agriculture Organization met to discuss this natural and economic disaster. The organization concluded that the introduction of the Nile perch failed to achieve its purpose. It noted that the population of economically-important cichlids was seriously threatened with extinction. It also noted that fish production in this area had decreased by 80 percent. Claims that disadvantages were compensated for by the greater value of the higher quality of fish caught were contradicted by prices that local people set for the perch.

Since 1984, many scientists have taken steps to prevent disasters of this kind. They know that the uncontrolled introduction of nonnative predators can lead to the disappearance of important fish species. When species disappear, their gene pools are lost forever. Local fish evolve over millions of years in unique local environments. The case of the Nile perch is seen as a failure by specialists who value various African fish for scientific reasons. It is also considered a failure by the people who were supposed to benefit from the program. Scientists hope that organizers of future projects will consult them before setting up similar programs.

Fish of the Marshes

Some freshwater areas of Africa are sites of very rapid evolutionary processes. In other area, waters are inhabited by primitive types of fish that could be called "living fossils." Examples of "living fossils" are found among ten spe-

Mudskippers inhabit coastal marshes. They are able to walk out of the water on their front fins. They take in oxygen from the air through their skin. Many marsh fish use similar adaptations to survive dry periods or conditions without water circulation.

ies of bichirs and reed fish. The species of these groups have long, eel-like bodies. Their bodies are covered by very hard, primitive types of scales. The first ray-finned fish on earth had these types of scales.

Bichirs and reed fish have a grayish green or yellowish brown color with spotted or striped patterns. Their colors make these fish hard to spot on a muddy bottom or among vegetation along lakeshores or riverbanks. They inhabit the Senegal, Volta, Niger, Congo, and Nile rivers, Lake Chad and Lake Rudolf.

The most characteristic feature among the bichirs and reed fish is the structure of the dorsal fin. The dorsal fin is the main fin located on the back. It is divided into a series of separate small fins that runs along the back from the head to the tail. These fin elements stand up straight when the fish swims. The structure of the pectoral fins, located below the gills, is also rather unusual. One section of the pectoral fins has a muscle and internal skeleton that supports the fish when it lies on the bottom of a river or lake. The bichirs' hind fins are small. The Calabar reed fish does not have hind fins.

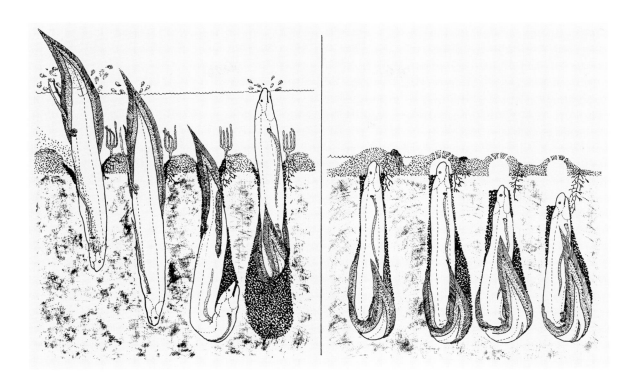

Hibernation processes of the African lungfish are shown in this drawing. In this species, the swim bladder is divided into two equal parts. These parts are comparable in structure and function to human lungs. During dry periods, the lungfish survives by burrowing a tunnel in the mud. It remains in its hole, encased by a layer of mucous, which keeps its skin moist. It breathes oxygen from the air by using its swim bladder.

Both bichirs and reed fish are carnivores. They hunt small fish and small invertebrates (animals without backbones). Both of these fish swim very slowly when hunting, but they dart away when fleeing from danger.

Another primitive characteristic of these fish is the open swim bladder. This feature was lost by other species when they began to inhabit deep water. In the deep water, it is necessary to have a closed swim bladder to offset the high pressure. Bichirs and reed fish use their open swim bladders as lungs for breathing. These fish are often found in muddy streams where oxygen is scarce. Whenever the fish are unable to obtain enough oxygen from the water, they breathe in air. By using this ability, bichirs and reed fish are able to survive the dry season while remaining hidden in mud. They also are able to move through the mud on land for a short time while searching for water.

After hatching, young bichir fish are able to survive in environments lacking oxygen. This ability comes from using special gills. Upon hatching, young bichirs have external gills that are like the gills of salamanders. These branched gills have many blood vessels. As young bichir fish mature, these gills disappear.

African otter

African fish owl

ruddy pelican

osprey

Some sort of adaptation that allows fish to breathe air is common among tropical fish that live in marshes and backwaters of muddy rivers.

Like some amphibians, mudskippers breathe air through their bare skin. Snakeheads have simple breathing organs in their throat cavities. Walking catfish of the genus *Clarias* have gill cavities that extend upward. These cavities are filled with branched breathing sacs with many blood vessels. The sacs form a very efficient type of "lung." These various adaptations enable these fish to survive suffocation, or drying out, during the dry season. During the dry season, they dig out an area in the mud. They remain in this area until the rains start falling.

Many of these fish, including mudskippers, snakeheads, and certain types of catfish, are also able to walk. These fish walk out of the water using their pectoral fins. During this movement, they keep their heads straight upward, away from the ground. The walking style of the West African mudskipper has been described in detail. When moving, the rays of the pectoral fins are used like crutches. The body weight is supported by the pelvic fins, the lower, rear fins near the tail. By moving this way, these fish are able to go from one pond to another. In the coastal marshes, they even are able to climb mangrove trees.

It was through adaptations such as these that the first amphibians evolved. Without these features, it would be impossible for fish to live even partially out of water.

Of all living fish, the lungfish are most closely related to amphibians. There are only five species of lungfish that inhabit tropical rivers. Three are found in Africa, one in South America, and one in Australia. African lungfish have lost the ability to walk on their fins. However, they are able to hibernate in mud due to a special lung. Their survival out of water also is aided by a blood circulation system that is like the system found in primitive land vertebrates (animals with backbones). As in bichirs and reed fish, their swim bladder opens into the throat cavity. In the African lungfish, the swim bladder is divided into two equal lobes. In bichirs and reed fish, one lobe of the swim bladder is much larger than the other. Like most fish in the world, the Australian lungfish has two unequal swim bladder lobes.

The Main Predators of Fish

Under natural conditions, fish in African waters are preyed upon by animals such as cormorants, pelicans,

and fish owls. Crocodiles lurk, and the African river eagle scans the water from above. This eagle is an outstanding symbol of African wildlife. It belongs to the group of sea eagles which includes the bald eagle. Like the bald eagle, the river eagle has a white head and tail. In the river eagle, however, the white color extends to the breast and the back. The rest of the body is brown, and the wings are black.

The river eagle is also a large bird. It measures about 3 feet (1 m) from head to tail. The male has a wingspan of a little over 6 feet (1.9 m). But the female's wingspan measures about 8 feet (2.5 m). The river eagle weighs from 4.4 to 6.6 pounds (2 to 3 kg). It can capture fish of its own weight. Although it normally prefers smaller prey, it readily preys on waterfowl.

Unlike many other birds of prey, the river eagle is not in danger of extinction. Its populations are still quite numerous. It is distributed over practically all of Africa south of the Sahara Desert. It does not live in the driest zones of Somalia, Kenya, and South Africa.

The characteristics and habits of the river eagle are well known because of research by the zoologist Leslie Hilton Brown. The total population has been estimated at

An African river eagle is fishing. This bird of prey often acts as a pirate, stealing fish away from other birds. Such behavior is successful because of this bird's impressive size and flying ability.

The colorful, marbled rush frog inhabits reed beds and marshes.

between 100,000 and 200,000 nesting pairs and 20,000 to 50,000 young individuals. In some areas, the population density of this bird is greater than one pair for every 984 feet (300 m) of riverbank or shoreline. Such a high density leaves virtually no free territories for young eagles to occupy.

One of the reasons that this particular species is so numerous is that its reproductive rate is higher than that of other birds of prey. In most species of birds of prey, two chicks are born to a nesting pair. Usually, the strongest chick kills the other chick or pushes it out of the nest. But among river eagles, it is common for both chicks to survive the nesting period.

As soon as the young eagles are able to provide for themselves, they are driven away from the territory of the parents. Young river eagles gather in groups in marginal areas. Here they live on refuse and animal carcasses. Eventually, they become strong and experienced enough to obtain their own territories. But only 20 percent of these young eagles reach sexual maturity, which occurs at the age of four or five years.

Distribution of the river eagle depends on the availability of natural environments and on activities of local people

in their territories. River eagles are not bothered as long as fishermen allow some fish to be lost from their catches. The species is safe if farmers do not spread poisonous pesticides on the land. Without human interference, this eagle continues to loudly proclaim its reign over Africa's fascinating lands.

African Amphibians

Several fish species have the ability to encase themselves in mud to survive dry periods. This ability is also typical of many amphibians. However, the only amphibians that are found south of the Sahara Desert are various species of frogs and toads. European salamanders and newts are not commonly found in Africa. This absence is balanced by the presence of several species of caecilians. Since they have no limbs, these strange animals look like large earthworms. The caecilians, however, are voracious predators. They eat worms, other amphibians, reptiles, and birds. Africa's largest species of caecilians exceeds 3 feet (1 m) in length.

African tree frogs, such as Peter's tree frog, are so tied to their tree environments that they lay their eggs in trees. Eggs are deposited in foamy masses and remain attached to branches. These branches are normally 6 feet (2 m) above the level of the water. As soon as they hatch, tadpoles fall from the trees.

CROCODILES AND MONITOR LIZARDS

Crocodiles are the largest living reptiles on earth. Twenty-three species of crocodiles, which are classified into three distinct families, occupy various areas of the continent today. They live in the tropical and subtropical regions of all the continents, excluding Europe. Of the African species, the Nile crocodile is the largest and also the best known. This animal was described by the Greek historian Herodotus in the fifth century B.C. It can reach a length of 16 to 20 feet (5 to 6 m) and a weight of 1,995 pounds (905 kg).

The Nile Crocodile

The Nile crocodile is one of the largest carnivores of tropical Africa. It has a unique body shape compared to other African carnivores such as lions, hyenas, and leopards. Its present "dragon-like" appearance has not changed much since ancient times.

In fact, modern crocodiles have many of the ancient features that characterized their ancestors that lived millions of years ago. These ancestors were giant reptiles and dinosaurs that dominated earth's freshwater environments. They reached a length of 50 feet (15 m) and a weight of several tons.

Until the beginning of this century, it was possible to sail down one of the large African rivers and find numerous groups of crocodiles along the way. Today, unfortunately, the majority of African rivers provide homes to only a limited population of these gigantic animals. Crocodile populations have been reduced greatly by extensive hunting. The skin of crocodiles is highly valued.

Murchison Falls National Park, on the Victoria Nile, is one of the few zones in which these reptiles are still abundant. Lake Rudolf is also home to numerous crocodiles. Because of the high level of mineral salts dissolved in the waters of Lake Rudolf, crocodiles there have large salt crusts on their bodies. This crust makes their skin lose most of its commercial value.

Nile crocodiles spend most of the day basking in the sun along river shores. Only in the hot southern areas do they seek out shade or briefly cool off in the water. These animals do not have sweat glands. They release excess heat by keeping their jaws open wide to permit evaporation from the moist lining of their mouths. Toward evening, they return to the water, where they spend the night.

Crocodiles feed and mate in the water. They eat car-

Opposite page: The Nile crocodiles are among the most specialized of the predators which live in slow-moving waters. Because of various adaptations, they have survived in these environments for ages. Crocodiles are one of the most ancient reptile forms on earth today. Only turtles have a longer history, and theirs precedes even the dinosaurs.

73

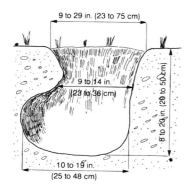

9 to 29 in. (23 to 75 cm)

9 to 14 in. (23 to 36 cm)

8 to 20 in. (20 to 50 cm)

10 to 19 in. (25 to 48 cm)

mongoose

marabou stork

goliath heron

casses of dead animals. In one instance, 120 crocodiles were counted next to a dead hippopotamus. After killing large prey, they hide it under the water and wait until it begins to decay. Only then will they tear it to pieces.

Nile crocodiles prey on several species of birds, most commonly ducks and geese. But other bird species are not harmed by these reptiles. Some birds even eat parasites off crocodiles' bodies without any danger of being attacked. These include the common sandpiper, the spur-winged lapwing, and, especially, the black-eyed courser, also called the "crocodile bird." The sandpiper and the crocodile bird even eat parasites from inside the crocodile's mouth without being attacked.

The stone curlew is another bird that is found in areas where crocodiles gather. This bird always nests near locations where crocodiles bury their eggs and watch over them. The stone curlew uses crocodiles as "watchdogs" for its own nest. As long as crocodiles are around, it is unlikely that small predators will dare to prey on curlews or steal their eggs.

The Reproduction of Crocodiles

The large male crocodiles which live along the shores of Lake Rudolf, in Kenya, are territorial. Females select mating partners according to the quality of their territories. The sunny areas and nesting sites in a given territory are factors that the female considers when choosing a mating partner.

Nile crocodiles actively care for their young. The female digs a hole about 8 to 20 inches (20 to 50 cm) deep in sand near the shore. During the night, she lays up to forty eggs in the nest hole and then covers the eggs with sand and grass. Females maintain the same nesting zones for years. They often build their nests only a few feet from each other.

The incubation, or hatching of eggs, takes from eleven to fourteen weeks. During this time, the mother constantly watches over her nest. She drives away predators that eat crocodile eggs, such as hyenas, baboons, marabou storks, mongooses, and Nile monitor lizards.

Just before hatching, the young make sounds and vibrate the shell of the egg. This is a signal to the mother that the eggs are about to hatch. When the mother hears the young, she uncovers the nest. The newly-hatched crocodiles measure 10 to 13 inches (26 to 34 cm) in length. Because of their small size, the young are easily preyed upon by Nile

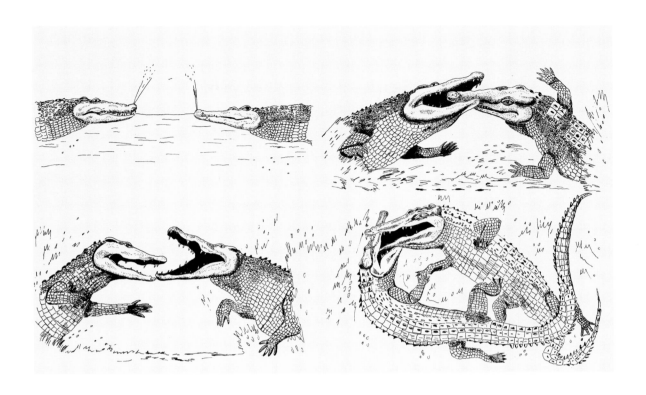

softshell turtles, sea eagles, marabou storks, and vultures. During the night, they are prey for the milky eagle owl. Some of the young are killed by diseases. Only 2 to 5 percent of the young in each nest reach the age of sexual maturity. This occurs even though the young are watched over and defended by their mother and by other females.

When unfavorable climatic conditions occur, crocodiles dig a large underground hole next to the water. Here they take shelter for long periods of time and go without eating until conditions are more favorable. The young spend much time in these holes before they are large enough to scare off predators.

At one time, scientists thought that crocodiles dug holes with their front feet. Later, they learned that they dig with their jaws. In the water, the crocodile digs the soft soil of the shore just above the waterline. It then submerges and shakes its head to the side, getting rid of soil held by the jaws. During the digging process, soil is deposited away from the hole that is being dug.

Other Species of African Crocodiles

The long-nosed crocodile lives in the rain forests of

Crocodiles spend many hours of the day with their jaws open. This is done to lower the animal's body temperature. The moist surface inside the mouth is the only part of the body that can release heat by evaporation of fluids. Several species of birds take advantage of these moments to gather fragments of food from between the teeth of these powerful reptiles. These birds thus serve a hygienic, or healthful, function.

Three other species of crocodiles are found in Africa, each smaller than the Nile crocodile. These are the long-nosed crocodile *(top)*, the broad-fronted crocodile *(bottom)*, and the Osborn's crocodile. Some zoologists consider the Osborn's crocodile to be a subspecies of the broad-fronted crocodile.

western Africa. It lives in an area that extends from the Senegal River in an eastern direction toward the Congo River, and in a southern direction toward Angola. This species also has been sighted along Lake Tanganyika. The long-nosed species of crocodiles that live along this lake rarely exceed 6 feet (1.8 m) in length.

The broad-fronted crocodile lives in a band of land that extends along the western side of Africa. This band includes the countries of Sierra Leone, Guinea, Ghana, Togo, Nigeria, Cameroon, and Gabon. Like the long-nosed crocodile, the broad-fronted crocodile is smaller than the Nile crocodile. It grows to a maximum length of slightly more than 6 feet (1.9 m). It has a surprisingly short snout and maroon eyes that usually turn blackish in adulthood.

Osborn's crocodile belongs to the same genus as the broad-fronted crocodile. Some scientists claim that these two animals are subspecies of the same species. Others believe they are two separate species. Osborn's crocodiles live 620 miles (1,000 km) away from the closest broad-fronted crocodiles. They live in northeastern Zaire, mostly in the Itimbri River. This tributary of the Congo River flows through a rain forest. The Osborn's crocodile is consider-

ably smaller than its western relative, growing to just over 3 feet (1 m) in length. Its habits are relatively unknown.

The Decline of the Crocodile

At one time, crocodiles were so numerous in Africa that they posed a threat to livestock. Even as recently as the early twentieth century, the Tanzanian government paid a bounty for each dead crocodile.

Today, crocodiles are in danger of extinction in Africa, as well as in other parts of the world. These animals are widely hunted for their skins. Large profits can be made in a short time from the sale of crocodile skins.

The Nile Monitor Lizards

One of the most noteworthy of Africa's reptiles is the Nile monitor lizard. This lizard is found throughout the area south of the Sahara Desert, reaching as far as Cape Province in South Africa. This lizard reaches a length of up to 6 feet (2 m) and can live up to fifteen years. Like all monitor lizards, the Nile monitor lizard is active during the day. Its strong legs enable it to run very quickly. It is also an excellent swimmer.

The Nile monitor is an enormous aquatic lizard that can reach a length of almost 6 feet (1.8 m) and is extremely agile. It swells up in case of danger. This makes its blue-and-yellow body look bigger than it really is.

79

HIPPO-POTAMUSES

The hippopotamus is one of earth's largest mammals. It is common and sometimes abundant in all of the lakes, ponds, rivers, and marshes of the African interior. This animal was called the "river horse" by ancient Greeks.

General Characteristics

The hippopotamus lived in ancient Egypt and Palestine. It has been well known for thousands of years. During ages when the climate was warmer, it lived in areas as far north as central Europe. About four thousand years ago, so many hippopotamuses lived along the lower course of the Nile River that they damaged cultivated crops. For this reason, they were widely hunted. A small group of hippopotamuses that survived in the Nile delta region until modern times became extinct at the beginning of the nineneeth century.

The hippopotamus has been further persecuted in the last two centuries. Today, it is distributed over an area from the northern edge of the Sahel to South Africa. It inhabits both lowland plains and elevations up to 6,560 feet (2,000 m) above sea level. It is found in all wetland environments, provided there are sufficient areas for pasturing.

The male hippopotamus has a length of about 10 to 14 feet (3.2 to 4.2 m). The female measures about 9 to 12 feet (2.8 to 3.7 m) in length. The male and female stand 4 to 5 feet (1.3 to 1.6 m) high at the shoulder. Each weighs from 2,865 to 7,055 pounds (1,300 to 3,200 kg).

The upper and lower jaws of these huge animals are equipped with impressive, curved canine teeth. These large teeth are visible when the hippopotamus challenges or threatens other animals. They are also visible when the animal is engaged in a fight.

Hippopotamuses are well adapted to living in water. Their ears and nostrils close while they are submerged. Their eyes are specially adapted for seeing under the water. Their skin is almost 2 inches (5 cm) thick. It was used in the past to make whips.

A newborn hippopotamus weighs about 110 pounds (50 kg). Young nurse for about one year. During the first six months of their lives, they gain about one pound of weight per day. The mother remains with her young long after the time of weaning. In fact, mothers and young stay together almost until the young reach sexual maturity. Females reach maturity at about nine years, and males reach maturity at about seven years.

Opposite page: Of all the large African mammals, the hippopotamus is the most directly dependent on the availability of water. One could call it an"amphibious" animal. In spite of its two to three tons of weight, this animal moves with agility both in the water and on land.

During the afternoon hours, hippopotamuses often leave the water to lay in the sun or to graze. However, the greater part of the day is spent in the water.

Male hippopotamuses can mate throughout the year. But females mate only once every two years. In Uganda, the majority of female hippopotamuses mate in either February or August. Births occur during the rainiest months of the year, when food is most plentiful. Both mating and birth occur in the water. Pregnancy lasts eight months. Young are able to nurse on their mothers' milk under the water within a few minutes after birth.

Hippopotamuses can live up to forty or fifty years. However, about 20 percent of young hippopotamuses die during the first year of life. Very few of these animals die from deadly diseases or parasites. The young of this species, however, are preyed upon by leopards, hyenas, and crocodiles. Adults have less to fear from these predators, but they are widely hunted by humans.

Group Life and Territoriality

Some of the most important studies on the hippopotamus have been carried out in the Queen Elizabeth National Park in Uganda. Hippopotamuses are very numerous in this

park. The park extends along the western side of the Rift Valley to the equator. It surrounds Lake Edward and Lake George with about 772 sq. miles (2,000 sq. km) of savannahs and wetlands. These two lakes are connected by the Kazinga Canal.

Many zones of the park have soils that originated from volcanic activity. This soil, along with regular rainfall and strong radiation from the sun, results in a high production of vegetation. Because of the abundance of vegetation, many animals live here. A large percentage of the total animal population consists of elephants, buffalo, and hippopotamuses.

Hippopotamuses are dependent on water, where they spend the majority of their time. They come onto land to feed, especially at night. During their nocturnal raids, they sometimes travel distances of 3 miles (5 km) away from the water. But they rarely move more than 5 miles (8 km) from the water. During the afternoon, hippopotamuses often leave the water to lay in the sun or eat grass. However, in many zones where they are disturbed, they avoid the land.

This photo shows the climax, or peak, of a fight between two hippopotamuses. Hippopotamuses are territorial animals. While fighting, males use their long and sharp canine teeth as weapons.

Hippopotamuses are most often found in shallow rivers with calm waters. They prefer areas where they can remain under the water as far as possible from the shore and where the young can drink without having to swim. If the young had to enter the water to drink, they would be easy targets for attacks by predators.

Hippopotamuses live in groups of ten to twenty individuals. Occasionally, however, they are found in larger groups of up to 150 individuals. These groups are usually casual gatherings in resting areas.

Adult males are territorial and occupy a well-defined territory in the water and on the shore. Males enjoy a sort of

"reproductive right" within these territories. Mating occurs only in a male's territory. Nonterritorial males are strictly excluded from the territories of other males. The males that occupy territories located on flat, sandy shores are particularly attractive to females. Consequently, these males have the greatest chances of mating.

A territory in an unsuitable part of the river can quickly change into attractive territory. This happens because of the action of river currents. River currents can move and deposit large amounts of sand over just a year or two. A territory ranges in size from 820 to 1,640 feet (250 to 500 m) along a lakeshore, and from 164 to 328 feet (50 to 100 m) along a river. A male may experience shore changes in his territory if he keeps the same territory for a period of several years. Two males observed in Lake Edward have occupied the same territory for at least eight years without interruptions.

Often, violent and ferocious fights take place along the edges of these territories. Two males confront each other at the border of their territories. They face each other at a distance of about 16 feet (5 m). They extend their ears forward and raise their snouts above the water surface. After a few minutes, they move around marking their territories, as many animals do, with bodily wastes. At the same time, they energetically move their tails around as if they were rotors. By doing so, they are able to scatter their dung over a distance of several feet. As soon as they are done with this action, each male draws away from the other and moves toward the center of his own territory.

A territorial male will tolerate the presence of several nonterritorial males, as long as his own mating rights are recognized. Males often mark their territories over and over in the same zones. This results in the formation of large piles of dung in one area. Socially inferior males, females, and young hippopotamuses respect these markings.

Hippopotamuses feed mainly on grasses. They require an average amount of 88 pounds (40 kg) of food per day. Studies of stomach contents of hippopotamuses living in Queen Elizabeth National Park indicate that these animals eat more than thirty species of grasses. The amounts of different grasses that they eat vary according to the period of the year. During dry periods, hippopotamuses frequent areas of the park where there is a constant supply of water. They occupy these areas even though these areas may not have abundant supplies of food.

During rainy periods, some of the hippopotamuses scatter to live in small ponds and marshes. Thus, when water is abundant and many small marshes are available, populations of hippopotamuses are more scattered. During dry seasons, populations are concentrated around a few permanent marshes.

Effects of Hippopotamus Populations on the Environment

Hippopotamuses affect vegetation. Small groups of these animals have been observed in areas where they gather to eat grasses. Here, the highest vegetation disappears and is replaced by shorter plants. The shorter plants are spread partly by *stolons*, which are stems that grow along or under the ground and take root to form new plants. The new, shorter vegetation can more easily withstand the effects of the grazing and trampling of these large animals than the taller vegetation can.

Hippopotamuses prefer grasses no higher than 6 inches (15 cm). They tear grasses by taking hold of them with their horny lips and then suddenly raising their heads. Often, entire clumps of grass are pulled up at one time, even the roots.

Hippopotamuses often use the same paths at night when they leave the water in search of food on land. As a result, they form trails. These trails consist of two ruts separated by a strip of vegetation in the middle. Along mountain slopes, these trails create runoff troughs for rainwater. Eventually these ditches are partially washed away by erosion.

Over time, hippopotamuses compact the soil. This causes the soil to lose its capacity to absorb water. It becomes more easily eroded. Resulting problems were subjects for bitter debates in the late 1950s. Ecologists, scientists who study natural environments, believed that eroded areas would become desert lands. To prevent this, ecologists decided that 50 percent of the hippopotamus population had to be killed. They designed a program of controlled killing for many areas.

None of the twelve thousand hippopotamuses that lived in the Queen Elizabeth National Park or in nearby Virunga National Park were killed at that time. Although environmental conditions of the two parks were similar to endangered areas, desert areas were not being formed in the these parks. But, eventually, the ecological balance within the parks proved that the ecologists made an unwise deci-

Before physically attacking each other in a confrontation, hippopotamuses open their jaws *(top and middle)*. This is done to intimidate, or frighten, the rival hippopotamus. If the rival does not immediately leave the territory, they attack each other ferociously *(bottom)*. While biting, they aim for the blood vessels in the neck and in the shoulder area. Sometimes their teeth produce deep wounds.

Pygmy hippopotamuses are one-tenth of the size of the common hippopotamuses. This species is more cautious than its larger relative. Small groups of pygmy hippopotamuses are active at dusk and during the night. At night, they walk from marshes to graze in the interior of forests.

sion. From the parks, the ecologists learned that animals do not destroy the environments which they inhabit. But during the killing of the hippopotamuses, local people learned to appreciate the taste of hippopotamus meat. During the killing period, large amounts of hippopotamus meat were distributed to the local people. When the hunting of this species was forbidden by law, the demand for hippopotamus meat did not stop. Poachers began to kill hippopotamuses for their meat.

In spite of poaching, the hippopotamus population made a comeback. During the next two decades, the population of this species reached its previous level. In 1979, after the expulsion of the Ugandan dictator Idi Amin, the hippopotamus population declined again. This decline was caused by massacres carried out by Tanzanian liberation troops who worked with Ugandan merchants. Today, the population of this species is recovering once more.

The Pygmy Hippopotamus

The pygmy hippopotamus is not as well known or as widespread as the common hippopotamus. It was described for the first time in 1841. A living example of this species was first transported to a European zoo in 1912.

The pygmy hippopotamus is found only in two small zones near the coast of western Africa. The species lives in

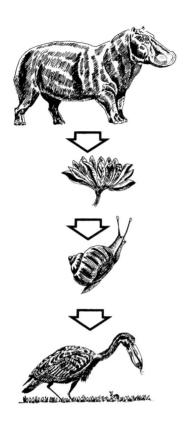

Hippopotamuses play an important role in freshwater environments. The manure they drop in the water fertilizes aquatic plants. Aquatic plants are food for amphibious snails. In turn, snails are a basic part of the diets of many birds, such as the African open-bill stork.

marshes where the major plants are palms and ferns. The plants of these marshes appear to be floating on the water in mats. Palm trees have many aerial roots growing up out of dark water. The water is up to 10 feet (3 m) deep.

Pygmy hippopotamuses live in such marshes but also enter nearby forests. Their movements create systems of trails that often end in clearings where there is an abundance of food. It is difficult to get close to pygmy hippopotamuses. Their habitat makes travel difficult for humans. And their sense of smell is so developed that they immediately know when strangers are near.

The pygmy hippopotamus is like the common hippopotamus, but it is smaller. It is about the size of a large pig. It is about 5 feet (1.5 m) long and weighs between 397 and 573 pounds (180 to 260 kg). It is about ten times smaller than an average-sized common hippopotamus.

Pygmy hippopotamuses are primarily active after sundown. Then they move in search of food. Normally, pygmy hippopotamuses move from marshes into forests every day. They graze for two to six hours, then return to their refuges. They use their large, curved canine teeth and two upper incisor teeth to tear vegetation. The males show these teeth as weapons when facing a rival, grinding them in a menacing way. In spite of their awkward bodies, pygmy hippopotamuses are able to stand on their hind legs. They can support themselves on trunks of palm trees to reach the leaves of tree ferns, which they are particularly fond of eating.

Unlike their larger relatives, pygmy hippopotamuses have varied diets. Their diets include leaves, roots, ferns, and fruit that falls to the ground. During each "raid" into the forest, each animal eats up to 22 pounds (10 kg) of plant substances. Pygmy hippopotamuses cannot digest the fibrous tissues, called "cellulose," of plants. Therefore, they must eat foods that have high nutritional value. After eating, animals return to their refuges, often taking different paths.

Like their larger relatives, pygmy hippopotamuses mark their territories with dung. In this species, even females display this behavior. The marking of territories is done in different ways. In some areas, dung may be completely absent. In others, it is deposited every 6 feet (2 m). Both male and female pygmy hippopotamuses are territorial and live alone. Studies show that they clearly mark their territories in areas where population density is high or when food, water, or resting areas are scarce.

Hippopotamuses play another important role in the slow-flowing African rivers. The continual passage of these massive animals keeps rivers free of floating vegetation. This action prevents the formation of floating mats of vegetation that clog river flow. Thus, rivers remain well drained.

Several violent fights have been observed between pygmy hippopotamuses in captivity. However, such fights have not been observed in the wild. In captivity, even mating can erupt into fighting. Fighting breaks out when animals that normally live alone seek to dominate a partner. As a result of such fights, almost all adults have scars from large wounds on their backs, necks, or sides.

It is not known how this species rears the young in the wild. However, observations made by local hunters indicate that a mother does not bring her young along when traveling daily into the forest. Offspring are left in the refuge until they reach a certain age. Thus, newborn young can be preyed upon easily by leopards, rock pythons, and Nile monitor lizards. The adult, however, has only two enemies, the leopard and the human.

The native people of Africa consider the meat of the pygmy hippopotamus a delicacy. And although it is against the law, organized hunts continue to kill the pygmy hippopotamuses.

THE INHABITANTS OF RIVERBANKS AND SHORES

Africa's bodies of water are surrounded by thick borders of vegetation and populated by a wide variety of insects. These aquatic environments are ideal habitats for many different types of birds.

Birds of the Sandy Shores

Along the sandbanks that line river courses, visitors often see the nests of kingfishers and bee-eater birds. The colonies of carmine bee-eaters along the Senegal and Niger rivers are particularly spectacular. Hundreds and sometimes thousands of these birds come and go from nests dug in the sand. The carmine bee-eater has a brilliant red color (carmine), a blue head, and a cobalt blue back. From afar, a flock of these birds looks like a red cloud in motion.

The red bee-eater is very similar to the carmine bee-eater. It is found along the Zambesi River and in the large lakes region of the Rift Valley. There are more than ten species of bee-eaters in Africa. All of them are characterized by bright colors that include different shades of green, yellow, and blue. The most common species is Muller's bee-eater. Normally, colonies of this species number several thousand nesting pairs.

These birds are tied to aquatic environments because of the large populations of insects that live there. Dragonflies are the most common insects living in aquatic areas. Bee-eaters are skillful fliers. They easily capture insects like dragonflies. The incubating chambers of bee-eaters' nests are covered with the remains of insects which have been eaten by their young.

Bee-eaters and kingfishers belong to the same ancient group of birds. These birds evolved unique characteristics. Bee-eaters look like multicolored butterflies. They are characterized by long, thin beaks and two tail feathers that extend beyond shorter tail feathers. Kingfishers are much stouter. Their large heads seem out of proportion to their bodies. They have long, wide beaks which they use to capture fish and other large prey.

There are about fifteen species of kingfishers in Africa. They range in size from the 4-inch (11 cm) pygmy kingfisher to the 16-inch (40 cm) giant kingfisher. Due to its widespread distribution, the black-and-white kingfisher is the most studied species. This animal is found everywhere on the continent, except the regions of the Sahara Desert. It builds a nest, using its beak as a pick, by digging a tunnel in bare embankments. The nest is large enough to hold the young

Opposite page: Shown is a colony of carmine bee-eaters. These brightly-colored birds nest along the sandy banks of rivers.

The wattled crane is the largest crane in Africa. Its distribution is divided into two zones. It nests in the marshes of Ethiopia and at the southern extremity of the Rift Valley.

and allow the adult to enter and turn around before exiting. One of the most remarkable characteristics of this species is that young males without territories often help other birds care for their young. It appears that these young male helpers do not belong to the same family as the nesting pair. As soon as newly-hatched chicks begin calling out for food, kingfishers frequently are visible hovering over the water in search of fish.

Often, sandbanks also are inhabited by swallows, but these birds are not as striking as bee-eaters or kingfishers. Swallows gather in dense colonies. Their nests are deep galleries dug in the sand. They feed mainly on swarms of insects found above the water.

Large Aquatic Birds

Vast marshes that form during the rainy seasons offer food and refuge to bird populations that are richer and more striking than those of riverbanks. It is impossible to describe in just a few sentences the astonishing richness of birds found in these environments.

In the marshes of the Ethiopian plateaus, visitors see

Typical birds of the African waters are *(from left to right):* a crowned crane, a spur-winged goose, a pair of pygmy geese, and an Egyptian goose.

Egyptian geese and wattled cranes, the largest and most impressive of the African cranes. In the marshes of Lake Chad and the Niger River basin, there are many African species of ducks, herons, storks, and other wading birds. The most common native species are the white-faced tree duck, the spur-winged goose, and the pygmy goose. Also common are the beautiful white goliath heron and the small green heron. Here visitors also see huge flocks of migrating birds from Europe.

The sacred ibis, the African wood ibis, the ruddy pelican, and the crowned crane nest in the basin of the Nile River. In favorable seasons, great numbers of cormorants and thousands of African pelicans appear. The main nesting areas of these birds are located farther east and south, on the islands of the Rift Valley's lakes.

These birds follow a main migratory route that runs along the Rift Valley from Eurasia to southern Africa. Some of these birds stop in marshes in the area of the Tropic of Cancer. There, populations of migrating birds mix with populations of local birds. An example of this occurs in the low valley of the Senegal River. This area is the main wintering home for three species of migrating ducks. The garganey

A large group of aquatic birds wanders on the shore of an African lake. Marabou storks, cormorants, and pelicans can be seen in the foreground.

teal and the pintail duck travel here from Eurasia. The white-faced tree duck travels here from Ethiopia. These three species have a total population of over 250,000 in this area. Many other bird species also are present, but they only account for 10 percent of the total population here.

This northern tropical region has a rainy season between July and October. In October and November, the lowlands are flooded. Lush growth of aquatic vegetation covers the entire area. Garganey teals and pintails arrive between October and November. It is during these two months that the population densities of garganey teals and pintail ducks peak. The white-faced tree duck arrives at the end of October, when its young are first able to fly long distances. During the period when all three species are present, they form enormous flocks. These flocks make up 90 to 100 percent of the migrating birds in this region during the day. At night, the birds scatter to find food. The three species make use of different areas of the marsh at different times. Use varies according to water depth and types of vegetation.

However, this use does not explain how this area is able to support hundreds of thousands of birds that do not reproduce there. The answer lies in the seasonal availability

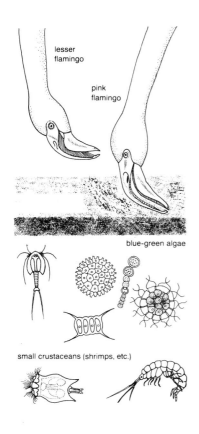

lesser
flamingo

pink
flamingo

blue-green algae

small crustaceans (shrimps, etc.)

The lesser flamingo and the pink flamingo are very numerous in lakes of the Rift Valley. Although they have the same type of downturned beak, they have different feeding habits. The beak assumes a horizontal position when the bird feeds under the water. The pink flamingo filters small aquatic animals from the muddy water at the bottom. The lesser flamingo, instead, feeds on microscopic blue-green algae near the surface.

of resources. Abundance in the habitat occurs at the time when migrating species arrive. Bird species that live year-round in the area do not reach high population levels. Their populations are limited by the dry seasons. During dry seasons, there is not enough food or habitat to support large populations of local species.

The Large Pink Population

Not all of the lakes of eastern Africa are as rich in life forms as Lake Tanganyika. Those found in very hot, dry areas receive little rainwater. Usually, the accumulation of rainwater does not equal the amount of water lost by evaporation. Under these conditions, mineral salts dissolved in the water become more and more concentrated. This results in a particular environment that is rich in salts and soda, or sodium carbonate. The high concentration of mineral salts prevents almost all higher forms of life from living in these waters. Lakes with this type of water condition are called "alkaline lakes."

Such environmental conditions are very favorable for the growth of blue-green algae and diatom algae. Diatom algae are single-celled, or colonial, algae. Their cell walls contain *silica*, a hard, glassy mineral. These algae multiply to such an extent that they transform alkaline lakes into vast expanses of green.

Only a few invertebrate animals are able to withstand as much salt and soda as alkaline lakes contain. The only source of food for them is microscopic algae. Some of the invertebrates found here are midges, which are small flies, and copepods, which are small crustaceans that swim with jerky, oarlike movements. Since they do not have other animals to compete with, copepods are extremely abundant.

Algae and invertebrates represent a rich food source for the few species of animals that are able to withstand high salt and soda waters. The most extraordinary of these animals are the flamingos. The two species that inhabit the alkaline lakes of Africa are the lesser flamingo and the common pink flamingo.

The pink flamingo is the better-known species, even to those who have not visited Africa. This spectacular bird also nests in the Mediterranean region, in the few areas where salty lagoons are found. In Europe, this bird feeds primarily on brine shrimp, which are very abundant in certain lagoons. In eastern Africa, its favorite food consists of midge larvae and copepods. Blue-green algae also make

The flamingos on the lakes of the Rift Valley sometimes number in the millions.

up a small part of its diet.

With its head upside down, the pink flamingo searches for food in the mud at the bottom of shallow water. It rapidly opens and closes its beak like a duck, while constantly moving its large, fleshy tongue. These movements bring large amounts of water, mud, and invertebrate animals in and out of its mouth. During this process, small invertebrates are separated from the water and mud mixture which is then expelled. Food is trapped by the numerous small blades lining the edges of the beak.

Lesser flamingos are more specialized than pink fla-

mingos. Lesser flamingos are found in Asia and in Africa. However, they are not found in Europe. They are smaller than common pink flamingos. But they have the same pink color. Unlike their larger relatives, lesser flamingos eat mainly blue-green algae and diatoms. They gather this from the top inch of the water of alkaline lakes.

The concentration of these extraordinary birds in eastern Africa is amazing. Half of the approximately four million flamingos existing in the world live only in the Rift Valley. During certain seasons, the majority of African flamingos may be concentrated only in Lake Nakuru.

GUIDE TO AREAS OF NATURAL INTEREST

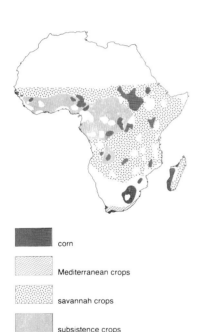

- corn
- Mediterranean crops
- savannah crops
- subsistence crops

Opposite page: The availability of drinkable water is one of the biggest problems facing a traveler on the African continent.

Above: The map shows some of the major uses of land in Africa. Quite a bit of land is still used for subsistence farming, which is the growing of food crops for a farmer's own use.

Africa offers visitors incomparable natural spectacles. But a visit to the humid plains and wetlands of the interior requires a certain number of precautions. Some of these relate to hygiene. Many insects that are common to the wetlands are carriers of extremely dangerous diseases, such as malaria and sleeping sickness. Before traveling to the interior, visitors should contact embassies, consulates, and tourist agencies of the various countries to obtain information about the recommended vaccines.

Visitors must also keep in mind that finding drinkable water in interior areas can be very difficult at times. To avoid parasites in the intestinal tract and worse illnesses, proper precautions should be taken before drinking from any bodies of water. However, it is not difficult to find food supplies or medical care.

In the past, in addition to the above risks, explorers also faced dangerous situations involving certain Arab merchants and warrior tribes. Several of the zones described in this book are off-limits to tourists since they are involved in wars or guerilla fighting.

These warlike situations also are harmful to the environment. For example, in recent years several of the most important national parks of Sudan have been abandoned because they are controlled by groups of armed rebels. For similar reasons, it is impossible to visit the Gombe National Park, located on the eastern shore of Lake Tanganyika. In addition, visitors must be aware that a large number of fires occur across the savannah during the dry season.

Fortunately, several African governments have become involved in the defense of their important natural heritage. This conservation awareness has developed only in recent years. The majority of Africa's national parks were established in the last decade. Some countries only recently moved toward protecting the environment. Nevertheless, their conservation efforts are ahead of European efforts. In Europe, only a few extremely important natural areas have been set aside.

There are many wetland areas of naturalistic interest in Africa. Almost all cover large areas. Visitors can enjoy a satisfying experience if they plan ahead and face inconveniences and discomforts with a spirit of adventure. They should be aware of the necessary vaccines and the political situations of the various countries. They are advised to turn to a specialized travel agency rather than be at risk for a simple oversight.

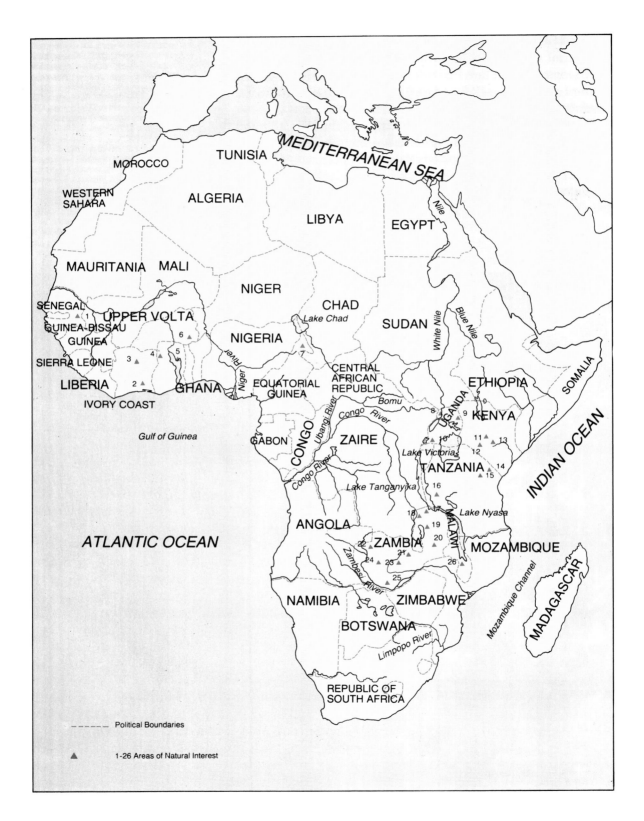

MEDITERRANEAN SEA

MOROCCO
TUNISIA
WESTERN SAHARA
ALGERIA
LIBYA
EGYPT

Nile

MAURITANIA   MALI
NIGER
CHAD
Lake Chad
SUDAN

SENEGAL   1
GUINEA-BISSAU   UPPER VOLTA
GUINEA   6
SIERRA LEONE   3   4   5
LIBERIA   2
IVORY COAST   GHANA   NIGERIA
Niger River

CENTRAL
AFRICAN
REPUBLIC
Bomu

White Nile   Blue Nile

ETHIOPIA
SOMALIA

Gulf of Guinea
GABON
CONGO
EQUATORIAL GUINEA
Ubangi River
Congo River
ZAIRE
Congo River

UGANDA   9   KENYA
8   10
11   13
Lake Victoria   12
TANZANIA   14
15
Lake Tanganyika   16

INDIAN OCEAN

ATLANTIC OCEAN

ANGOLA
Lake Nyasa
18   17   MALAWI
19
20
ZAMBIA   22   21
Zambezi River   24   23
25   26   MOZAMBIQUE

NAMIBIA
ZIMBABWE
BOTSWANA
Limpopo River

Mozambique Channel
MADAGASCAR

REPUBLIC OF
SOUTH AFRICA

- - - - - -   Political Boundaries

▲   1-26 Areas of Natural Interest

SENEGAL

Niokolo-Koba (1)

This is one of the largest national parks of western Africa, occupying an area of over 3,475 sq. miles (9,000 sq. km). It was established in 1954. Gradually, more area was added from a surrounding forest which was previously protected as a hunting reserve. The park contains various environments. These environments are distributed at different heights over hills and terraces. From May to October, hills are separated by low plains that are flooded by the Gambia River. The Gambia is the only river in the entire region that flows all year. Its tributaries, Niokolo-Koba and Koulountou, have no water during the dry season. The dry season lasts from November to May, following the typical seasonal changes of the Sudanese savannah. The major type of vegetation indicates that the park is located in a transitional zone. It ranges from open grassland and wooded savannah, with a variable tree covering, to a gallery forest. This forest is one of the typical forests found throughout Guinea. The predominant vegetation consists of cola nut and jujube trees.

A total of about seventy species of mammals live in the park. These include more than eight hundred hippopotamuses, caracals, pangolins, and aardvarks. There are 329 species of birds, 20 species of amphibians, 36 species of reptiles, including 3 crocodile and 4 turtle species. More than 60 types of fish live in the park's rivers and marshes.

IVORY COAST

Asaguy (2)

This region of 66 sq. miles (170 sq. km) is located between the mouth of the Bandama River and the Ebrie Lagoon. It is managed as a wildlife reserve for the protection of numerous species of monkeys and, especially, the African manatee, a seal-like, aquatic mammal. The monkeys live toward the interior of the palm forest, while the manatees inhabit coastal waters.

About three-fourths of this reserve's territory is covered with various types of marshes and swamps. Toward the ocean coast, these marshes are mixed with coastal mangrove swamps. Various species of crocodiles and an enormous number of aquatic birds are found in the reserve's marshes and swamps.

Access for tourists is rather difficult. However, visitors can reach the park by hovercraft from Abidjan or by crossing the lagoon by boat from Dabou-Grand. This town is located north of the reserve. There are no passable roads within the park. The closest lodgings are found at Grand-

Opposite page: Location of the most important wetland areas of natural interest in Africa.

Zebras gather in a marsh. The
importance of the floodplains has been
understood by many African
governments.

Lahou, beyond the Bamenda River. There is a camping area here equipped with facilities.

Northeast of Katiola, farther uphill along the Bandama River, visitors find a vast plateau with a climate typical of Sudan and Guinea. The area is covered by a vast savannah that is interrupted only by gallery forests. These forests grow along the tributaries of the main river. The various species of trees that grow here belong primarily to the bean and the white mangrove families.

The Haut-Bandama Nature Reserve is located in this zone. It extends over an area of 475 sq. miles (1,230 sq. km). Some of the animals that make their homes in the park include elephants, buffalo, and various species of antelope. The antelope species includes waterbucks, kobs, oribises, duikers, and reedbucks.

Haut-Bandama (3)

GHANA

Buy (4)

Buy National Park is located 248 miles (400 km) from Ghana's western border of the Ivory Coast toward the heart of western Africa. The park covers a total area of over 800 sq. miles (2,070 sq. km). It includes a large part of the upper basin of the Black Volta River. In the center of the park, a dense system of small tributaries flows into this river.

The typical vegetation alternates between savannah and gallery forests. The animal population is rich and varied. It includes antelope, baboons, and hippopotamuses.

Digya (5)

This national park covers 1,206 sq. miles (3,125 sq. km). It occupies a peninsula that juts out into Lake Volta from the western shore. The area has a savannah-type of vegetation with gallery forests along the principal streams. Among the animals of this park are many monkeys and large herbivores such as elephants and hippopotamuses. Crocodiles are also present.

Tourist facilities are not available in this park.

UPPER VOLTA

Arly (6)

This marshy wetland area covers 293 sq. miles (760 sq. km). It is found near the southeastern border of the country, where it connects with the Pendjari National Park of Benin. It has been a totally protected reserve since 1954.

The wetland is characterized by the presence of small lakes. The vegetation consists primarily of a Sudanese-type of wooded savannah. This changes to a gallery forest along the Pendjari River.

Large animals are the main attractions in this park. These include elephants, buffaloes, hippopotamuses, and various species of antelope, such as waterbucks and kobs. Predatory wildcats also are found here. Guenon monkeys and patas monkeys inhabit the forest.

The park, which is 186 miles (300 km) from Ouagadougou, is visited by thousands of tourists every year.

CAMEROON

Kalamaloué (7)

This natural park is located along the Chad border in the territory of Cameroon. It occupies 174 sq. miles (450 sq. km). It is a small park, but it is very important from a naturalistic standpoint. It is located in a lowland plain which becomes flooded in the wet season. This zone is an important refuge for crocodiles and wetland antelope.

Aquatic birds here include a rich variety of herons, storks, ducks, and kingfishers. There are also many African river eagles. Because of its bird populations, this park is well known for its favorable bird-watching conditions.

UGANDA

Ajay (8)

This reserve occupies almost 61 sq. miles (158 sq. km) along the western bank of the Nile River. It includes large areas of savannah and grassland, mixed with marshes along the river.

The Ajay Reserve was established in 1936 to protect the local population of white rhinoceroses. A staff of rangers continuously monitors this population. All of the animal species in the park are protected, including elephants, hippopotamuses, and kobs. The environment of this reserve is ideal for animals that typically inhabit wetland plains.

Pian-Upe (9)

With an area of about 891 sq. miles (2,310 sq. km), Pian-Upe is one of the largest reserves in Uganda. However, it is disturbed by several human activities, such as controlled hunting and the pasturing of livestock. The animal populations are counted periodically.

The reserve covers a vast plateau, drained by numerous streams that flow west into Lake Kyoga. The richness of the water supports a wooded savannah-type of vegetation along with some true forest areas.

There is a large variety of mammals within the reserve, including kobs, waterbucks, oribises, Grant's gazelles, giraffes, buffaloes, and zebras. The most remarkable birds here include ostriches, secretary birds, and yellow-beaked shrikes.

The area of the reserve ranges in elevation from 3,281 to 10,066 feet (1,000 to 3,068 m). Animal species typical of high elevations are found here, such as the mountain reedbuck antelope.

The park can be reached from Mbale or Moroto. Both are about 62 miles (100 km) away. There are no organized tourist facilities in the park. However, the beauty of the area and the ease with which the animals can be seen make a visit worthwhile.

Mburo Lake (10)

The region of Mburo Lake is the site of a reserve of 269 sq. miles (697 sq. km). It has been partially protected since 1959. Since 1964, further human settlements have been forbidden in this region. The reserve is marshy. It forms part of a larger complex of important wetland zones that includes two lakes. Marsh-type vegetation is present, with extensive beds of papyrus, reeds, and water lilies surrounding the open water. The dry areas are covered by an acacia-type of savannah.

The most evident and interesting large animals of this region are the many species of antelope. These include reedbucks, blesboks, and impalas. Leopards, warthogs, zebras, and hippopotamuses are also present. Controlled hunting is allowed in the reserve, but permission must be obtained from the appropriate authorities.

KENYA

Lake Nakuru (11)

Lake Nakuru is located in the center of Kenya, 87 miles (140 km) northwest of Nairobi. This lake is famous for its extremely high concentration of lesser flamingos and pink flamingos. The area became a national park in 1967. It was established with the aim of protecting the impressive populations of flamingos.

The park occupies a rather small area, about 22 sq. miles (57 sq. km). But it is large enough to include all of Lake Nakuru. The lake is an extremely important habitat for the pink birds. Lake Nakuru is actually quite shallow and is located in the main branch of the Rift Valley. Its waters are so strongly alkaline that only microscopic species of plant and animal organisms can survive in it. Algae are very abundant here and give the lake a strong green color. The abundance of microscopic algae sustains a large population of flamingos. Other aquatic birds, such as cormorants, pelicans, night herons, rare African spoonbills, and various species of wading birds, are also found in this park.

The rest of the park is covered by grassland. This is due to the residual salts left by the lake. This area is rich with plant-eating animals that are only found in this part of the world. There are two species of reedbucks. One is the Chanler's mountain reedbuck, which can climb the steep slopes of the Rift Valley. Typical aquatic animals include otters and hippopotamuses.

Aberdare (12)

This national park is located in the western region of Mount Kenya. It has an area of 296 sq. miles (766 sq. km). It includes the mountain group that forms the western wall of the Rift Valley. The two main peaks are Oldonyo Lasatiem at 13,104 feet (3,994 m) tall and Kinangop at 12,815 feet (3,906 m) tall. These peaks are separated by an alpine moor with an elevation of over 9,842 feet (3,000 m).

The mountain slopes are crossed by numerous torrents and streams. These streams cut across the forest as they flow to the valley below. On the alpine meadows, sedges and fescue grasses grow. Below the meadow, tree heaths, bamboo, podocarp trees, cedars, and olive trees grow. Other characteristic plants of these high altitudes include tree senecios and giant lobelias.

These forests are inhabited by blue guenon monkeys and numerous other species of mammals and birds. Black rhinoceroses and bongos live in the open zones. The small bongo antelope has a population of about two thousand in this area. In addition, the park is known to have a number of different environments. The various environments are useful in attracting a wide variety of bird species.

Mount Kenya (13)

The mountains that make up Mount Kenya are part of a volanic shield. This shield and the Rift Valley were formed at the same time. There are eight peaks in the park that reach elevations of over 15,420 feet (4,700 m). The highest peak is Mount Batian with an elevation of 17,058 feet (5,199 m). The national park covers an area of 276 sq. miles (716 sq. km). It contains numerous small lakes at elevations between 12,795 and 14,764 feet (3,900 to 4,500 m).

The environment of this region is very unusual. It includes an African type of alpine vegetation and typical species of mountain animals. The most characteristic plant community is the bamboo forest, which grows at elevations of 7,546 feet (2,300 m) and higher.

The Ngorongoro Crater in Tanzania is an impressive sight.

TANZANIA

Kilimanjaro (14)

Lake Manya (15)

Katari (16)

This national park is located on Mount Kilimanjaro and covers an area of 290 sq. miles (751 sq. km). It ranges in elevation from 6,004 feet (1,830 m) to 19,317 feet (5,888 m), which corresponds to the peak of Kibo. The area is part of a large volcanic complex. There are three inactive volcanoes in the park: Shira at 13,123 feet (4,000 m), Mawenzi at 16,893 feet (5,149 m), and Kibo at 19,340 (5,895 m) feet. Kibo is the only volcano that still shows a small amount of smoking activity. The mountain slopes are covered by a beautiful rain forest. Generally, the sides exposed to the south have humid woods of podocarp trees and tree ferns. The woods have a rich undergrowth of fern plants. The slopes facing north are covered with cedars and olive trees.

There is a considerable variety of animals, including various species of monkeys, wildcats, and large herbivores. An interesting species of duiker antelope is found only in this mountain zone. In addition, there are several species of birds, including two starling varieties that are native to the region.

Sixty-nine miles (112 km) from Arusha, on the road to Ngorongoro, visitors encounter the west wall of the Rift Valley. This is the boundary of Lake Manya National Park. The lake is found at the bottom of the Rift Valley. The park covers an area of 125 sq. miles (325 sq. km), most of which is occupied by this salty lake.

The park includes some forest areas, two small rivers that fall into the lake, and a towering wall that borders the great fracture. Several hot springs gush out from this wall. Many palm trees grow in the most humid areas. Several species of acacia shrubs form scrub areas where the ground is drier.

The park is well known for its populations of lions and black rhinoceroses. The park is also known for its numerous birds. At times, millions of pink and lesser flamingos arrive in this area all at once. There are many other species of aquatic birds in the park, as well as forty-four species of birds of prey.

At only 25 miles (40 km) from Mpanda on the road leading to the border with Zambia, visitors find this national park of 869 sq. miles (2,250 sq. km). It is located in a plateau area and includes parts of Lake Katari and Lake Chad.

Both of these lakes are connected to the Katuma River.

There is a vast system of marshes in the park. The waters of these marshes eventually drain into Lake Rukwa. Trees of the *Brachystegia* and *Isoberlinia* genera dominate and are especially abundant in the moist northern part of the park.

Hippopotamuses and crocodiles are common in this area. There are large numbers of pelicans and at least four hundred species of aquatic birds. In dry areas, large numbers of antelope, zebras, elephants, buffalos, and predatory cats live.

There are no lodgings available in the park except for a small camping area. Supplies are not available either. Visitors must be entirely self-sufficient.

ZAMBIA

Sumbu (17)

Like all of the African parks, the Sumbu National Park is relatively new. It was established only in 1972. This park includes a rocky shoreline along the southwestern side of Lake Tanganyika. The park protects an area of about 772 sq. miles (2,000 sq. km). Valleys that lead to the lake are dominated by acacia trees and *Trichilia* roka trees. A gallery forest grows along rivers that feed the lake.

There is an enormous variety of mammals here, including elephants, zebras, leopards, lions, buffaloes, various species of duikers, waterbucks, reedbucks, and roan antelope. Gulls, terns, and skimmer birds fly over the lake. Water cobras swim in the lake.

Mweru Wantipa (18)

This national park is a wide band of territory located in the area between Lake Mweru and Lake Tanganyika. Its appearance completely changes twice a year. The park covers an area of 1,208 sq. miles (3,130 sq. km), almost half of which consists of marshes and reed beds. Marsh vegetation disappears under the water when the area is covered by waters of Lake Mweru. The water level falls in the dry season. This flooding normally occurs once a year, although it is not extremely regular.

This unique environment offers the necessary conditions to support a rich and complex animal community. The animals include numerous species of antelopes, along with sitatunga antelope, black rhinoceroses, hippopotamuses, zebras, leopards, and lions. Crocodiles are found in the lake and rivers. The most spectacular birds are pelicans, various species of herons, shoebill storks, and an enormous number of flamingos.

There is a seasonal fishing village on the lakeshore. A

Sacred ibises are spotted in flight. A tremendous number of aquatic birds take advantage of the protected wetland areas. Every year, the local bird populations are increased by a large number of migrating birds that arrive here from Europe and Asia.

permanent village exists near the road that divides the park in two. The village is located in a wooded savannah area. The park can be reached only by one road.

Isbangano (19)

This national park of 324 sq. miles (840 sq. km) includes the northeastern edge of Lake Bangweulu's plain. The park is periodically flooded. A forest of padauk trees grows in this area. Papyrus plants and reeds grow along streams and rivers.

The unusual animals of this park include black lechwes and a rare species of reedbuck. Bird species include herons, ibises, and geese, which inhabit rivers where crocodiles swim. The Isbangano National Park is often hard to visit. For most of the year, it can only be reached by boat or on foot. There are no lodgings available.

North and South Luangwa (20)

Two national parks are found along the Luangwa River. One is located on the upper course of the river. It extends westward toward the cliff of Muchinga. The other is found east of the Luangwa River, at the same latitude as Lusaka.

The first park extends over an area of 1,787 sq. miles (4,630 sq. km). The second covers an area of 3,494 sq. miles (9,050 sq. km). Savannah vegetation in these parks varies according to different types of soil. River forests grow in suitable areas.

The valley of the Luangwa River is formed in a rift in the earth's crust. The plain at the bottom of the valley is humid and surrounded by steep slopes. It is an ideal habitat or environment for many mammals. Antelope are particularly numerous in this area. They are represented by a large number of species. The river offers a suitable habitat for hippopotamuses and crocodiles. This is one of the most important environments for the survival of these two animals. Bird populations are extremely rich. They include some large colonies of carmine bee-eaters.

Access to both parks is strictly regulated. These two parks can be entered only on foot. Vehicles are restricted to one part of the larger southern park. Lodgings are available from June to October only in the southern park.

Blue Lagoon (21)

This national park of 173 sq. miles (450 sq. km) is located at the northern edge of the Kafue River plain. It was established in 1973 on the site of a private ranch. The southern part of the park includes the Luwato lagoon. This is a large, slow-flowing branch of the Kafue River. The lagoon dries up only at the end of the dry season. During the rainy season, its waters swell to cover 30 percent of the park's surface area.

During the wet season, vegetation includes wild rice and papyrus. It grows near the river. Further away from the river, grasslands and a wooded savannah with acacias grow.

The most common carnivore in this zone is the African hunting dog. The park is home to several herbivores, such as zebras, kudus, and a large number of other antelope. A subspecies of lechwe antelope is native to the region. About 25,000 of these animals live within the park most of the year. The area facing the lagoon is an important feeding area for a large number of aquatic birds. Eastern glossy ibises and spur-winged geese feed here.

The park is 56 miles (90 km) west by road from the Lusaka-Mumbwa highway. Visitors also can arrive by aircraft, as there is a landing strip nearby. Overnight stays are possible only at a designated campsite. There are no services available for tourists.

Liuwa (22)

The Liuwa National Park is located on a plateau by the same name, at an elevation of 3,281 feet (1,000 m). Its total protected area extends over 1,413 sq. miles (3,660 sq. km). The park area is very flat and sandy. It is bordered on the east by the Luambimba River and on the west by the Luanginga River.

Periodic overflowing of these rivers forms marshes that are inhabited by lechwes. Buffalo and other species of antelope frequent the area. Crowned cranes and wattled cranes nest here.

Kafue (23)

Zambia has a network of nature reserves, several of which are very large in area. The largest of all is the Kafue National Park. It occupies a total area of 8,648 sq. miles (22,400 sq. km). It is located on a slightly rolling plateau which is crossed by the Kafue River and its two main tributaries, the Lufupa and the Lunga rivers.

A permanent marsh is found at the extreme northwestern corner of the park. It is connected to the Lufupa River by the wetland areas of the Busaga Plain. These wetlands result from the flooding of the Lufupa River. Other wetland areas of various sizes are scattered along the Kafue River and its tributaries.

The abundant water creates an ideal habitat for water-bucks, reedbucks, and lechwes, as well as for many populations of aquatic birds. Numerous other animal species that are not associated with wetland environments live in areas nearby.

Lochinvar (24)

This national park of 158 sq. miles (410 sq. km) is very similar to the Kafue National Park. It was formed in 1972 from land owned as a private ranch. Lochinvar National Park is located in the Kafue River Plain.

The flooding process begins suddenly in December. Floodwaters reach their maximum level in May and then gradually fall until November. This flooding favors the growth of rich aquatic and semiaquatic vegetation. Some of the most common plants found here are wild rice, *Vossia cuspidata*, cockspur grass, and panic grass.

Numerous herds of animals live in this park, including 35,000 Kafue lechwes. About four hundred species of birds also live here. Birds include white pelicans, pink-backed pelicans, goliath herons, African river eagles, and wattled cranes.

Mosi-oa-Tunya (25)

Victoria Falls is one of the most remarkable natural formations in Africa. The falls are created by the Zambesi River, near the southern border of Zambia. Part of the spectacular waterfall is located in the Mosi-oa-Tunya Park. This part covers an area of 25 sq. miles (66 sq. km) along the left bank of the Zambesi River. The park includes a series of deep gorges under the cascades.

During the period of highest water flow, March to April, 142 million gallons (540 million liters) of water per minute fall over Victoria Falls. The water drops 354 feet (108 m), spraying the vegetation at the base of the falls. This vegetation responds to the high humidity from the water spray. A dense forest rich with ferns grows here. In other areas along the Zambesi River, a thin band of river forest grows.

Animals of the river plain include elephants, buffalo, and antelope. A large community of perching birds inhabits the unique rain forest near the falls.

MALAWI

Liwonde (26)

Important concentrations of wild animals are found in this national park. Its area of 224 sq. miles (580 sq. km) includes the upper course of the Shire River and the land east of it. Numerous animals are present here, including lions, leopards, elephants, hippopotamuses, buffalo, and waterbucks. A small population of Nile crocodiles inhabits the river. In addition, an estimated 207 species of mostly aquatic birds live here.

The plant communities that grow here are very interesting. The area includes seven different plant zones, characterized by various groups of dominant plants. The first zone begins at the riverbank, and the others follow in a direction away from the river. Along the Shire River and on the shores of Lake Malombe, the plants are those which are typical of floodplains. In several places, gallery forests grow. Away from the river, a palm savannah is followed by a wooded savannah.

Liwonde Park was established in 1973, but it was not open to the public until 1978. Only day visits are permitted. Since 1974, this park has been the headquarters of important research conducted by the University of Malawi. This research focuses on changes in populations of the park's most interesting animal species.

Following pages: Elephants drink water in the Ninzima Springs National Park of Tsavo, Kenya.

GLOSSARY

acacia any of several trees, shrubs, or other plants of the legume family, with clusters of yellow or white flowers.

algae primitive organisms which resemble plants but do not have true roots, stems, or leaves. Algae are usually found in water or damp places.

alpine growing in high altitudes above the timber line.

altitude the height of a thing above the earth's surface or above sea level.

arid lacking enough water for things to grow; dry and barren.

atmosphere the gaseous mass surrounding the earth. The atmosphere consists of oxygen, nitrogen, and other gases, and extends to a height of about 22,000 miles (35,000 km).

basin all the land drained by a river and its branches.

bract a leaf, usually small or scalelike, sometimes large and brightly colored, growing at the base of a flower or on its stalk.

carnivore a meat-eating organism such as a predatory mammal, a bird of prey, or an insectivorous plant.

cataract any strong flood or rush of water; a waterfall.

cellulose the chief substance composing the cell walls or fibers of all plant tissue.

conifer cone-bearing trees and shrubs, most of which are evergreens.

conservation the controlled use and systematic protection of natural resources, such as forests and waterways.

continent one of the principal land masses of the earth. Africa, Antarctica, Asia, Europe, North America, South America, and Australia are regarded as continents.

crustacean a marine invertebrate characterized by a segmented body, hard outer skeleton or shell, and paired, jointed limbs. Lobsters, crabs, shrimps, and barnacles are crustaceans.

debris the scattered remains of something broken or destroyed.

ecology the relationship between organisms and their environment. The science and study of ecology is extremely important as a means of preserving all the earth's life-forms.

environment the circumstances or conditions of a plant or animal's surroundings. The physical and social conditions of an organism's environment influence its growth and development.

erosion natural processes such as weathering, abrasion, corrosion, etc., by which material is removed from the earth's surface.

germinate to sprout or cause to sprout, grow, or develop. Plant colonization begins with germination.

gill the saclike organ used for breathing by most animals that live in water, such as fish, clams, and lobsters.

habitat the area or type of environment in which a person or other organism normally occurs. Specific environmental factors are necessary for providing a "natural" habitat for all living things.

heath an extensive tract, or stretch, of open, uncultivated land covered with herbage and low shrubs. The soil of heaths is sandy and pebbly.

herbivore an animal that eats plants.

humid containing a large amount of water or water vapor.

humus a brown or black substance resulting from the partial decay of plant and animal matter.

lichen primitive plants formed by the association of blue-green algae with fungi. Lichens cover many of the tree trunks in Africa's rain forests.

lithosphere the solid, rocky part of the earth's crust. The earth's lithosphere is about 50 miles (80 km) deep.

mammal any of a large class of warm-blooded, usually hairy, vertebrates whose offspring are fed with milk secreted from special glands in the female.

mantle the layer of the earth's interior between the crust and the core. The continental plates float on top of the heavy rock of the earth's upper mantle.

moor a tract of open, rolling wasteland, usually covered with heather and often marshy or peaty.

musk a substance with a strong, penetrating odor secreted by some animals.

nocturnal referring to animals that are active at night.

omnivore an animal that eats both plants and other animals.

organism any individual animal or plant having diverse organs and parts that function as a whole to maintain life and its activities.

papyrus a tall water plant of the sedge family, abundant in the Nile region of Egypt.

parasite an organism that grows, feeds, and is sheltered on or in a different organism while contributing nothing to the survival of its host.

peninsula a land area almost entirely surrounded by water and connected with the mainland by a narrow strip of earth called an "isthmus."

ravine a long, deep hollow in the earth's surface, especially one worn by the action of a stream.

refuge a shelter or protection from danger or difficulty.

reserve land set apart for a special purpose. The many nature reserves of Africa are the government's effort to preserve its rich plant and animal resources.

rift an opening caused by splitting; a fissure.

savanna a treeless plain or a grassland characterized by scattered trees, especially in tropical or subtropical regions having seasonal rains.

sedimentary rock rock formed from sediment or from transported fragments deposited in water. Sedimentary rocks are formed from loose particles left by water or by sand which eventually accumulate and hold together.

silt sedimentary material consisting of fine mineral particles close in size to sand and clay. In deep water, where there is less movement, the tiny particles sink and settle to the bottom, forming layers of silt.

snout the projecting nose and jaws, or muzzle, of an animal.

solidify to make or become solid, firm, hard, or compact.

species a distinct kind, sort, variety, or class. Plant and animal species have a high degree of similarity and can generally interbreed only among themselves.

terrace a raised, flat mound of earth with sloping sides.

tributary a small stream or river which eventually flows into a large body of water.

zooplankton floating, often microscopic sea animals.

INDEX

CREDITS

MAPS AND DRAWINGS. A. Pilotto, Peschiera del Garda (Verona, Italy) G. Vaccaro, Cologna Veneta (Verona, Italy). **PHOTOGRAPHS. A. Borroni,** Milan: M. Mairani 8, 15. **Overseas,** Milan: Jacana/A. Bertrand 104-105; Jacana/M. Fievet 42; Jacana/J. Robert 90; Jacana/J.P. Varin — A. Visage 50-51, 54-55; Jacana/A. Visage 46-47; NHPA/A. Bannister 35, 82-83; NHPA/A.P. Barnes 36; NHPA/S. Krasemann 58, 98-99; NHPA/I. Polunin 66; NHPA/S. Robinson 79, 84-85, 116-117; NHPA/P. Scott 92; Oxford Scientific Films/A. Bannister 37; Oxford Scientific Films/G.I. Bernard 40, 48, 80; Oxford Scientific Films/M. Chillmaid 96; Oxford Scientific Films/M.J. Coe 71; Oxford Scientific Films/R. Coombes 69; Oxford Scientific Films/M.P.L. Fogden 70; Oxford Scientific Films/J. Paling 94-95; Oxford Scientific Films/D. Simonson 24; Oxford Scientific Films/D. Thompson 32-33; S. Osolonski 6-7. **Panda Photo,** Rome: 100; H. Ausloos cover; G. Cappelli 76-77; E. Coppola 17; A. Petretti 110-111. **D. Pellegrini,** Milan: 23, 26, 56-57, 120-121. **L. Pellegrini,** Milan: 11, 12-13, 14, 38-39, 44-45, 60-61, 72. **F. Veronesi,** Milan: 20-21, 30-31, 64-65, 89.

DATE DUE

Printed
in USA